MW01595983

Accidental Sailor Girl
—A Story of Growing

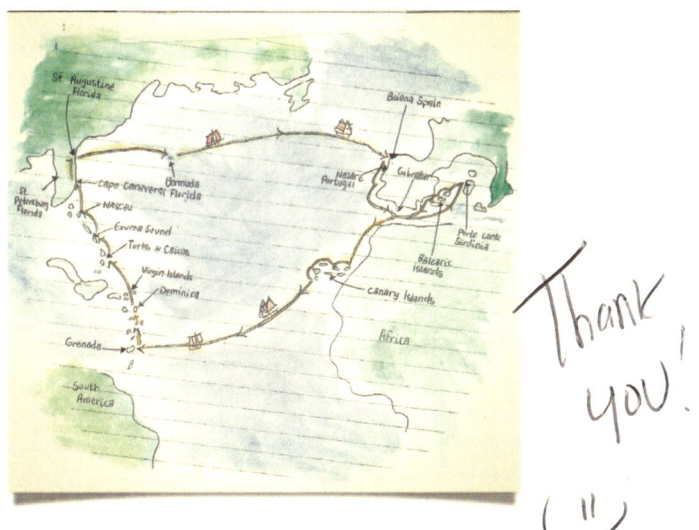

By Kourtney Patterson

Thank you! (")

"When I am old I'll tell you a story, but now that I'm young, I must live one..."
—Pete Grundvig

- To dad and Brynn

Paper Sailor Inc.

PO Box 676
Flagler Beach FL 32136

Library of Congress Control Number: 2014908912

ISBN - 10: 0990369803

ISBN - 13: 978-0-9903698-0-6

Printed in the United States of America

Chapter One
International Alphabet
-Bermuda

"D as in...dog, 2, C as in cat, cat, 7, 3, 1, alpha, elephant, Y as in yak, 6, kangaroo, frog, delta, over." I looked at my boyfriend Pete's amused expression, and I knew we were going to laugh about this later. We had not been to Bermuda before and we obviously did not know the International Phonetic Alphabet. This verbal alphabet is used to ensure that what is said over the radio is correctly heard. I made a

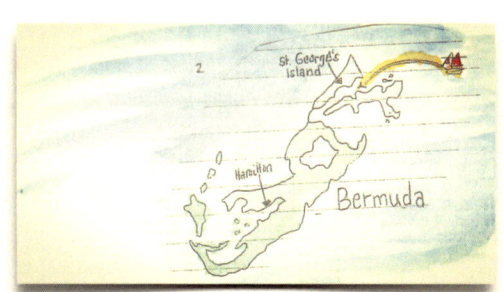

mental note to myself that I was going to memorize this alphabet on the next leg of our journey.

Suddenly, Bermuda Radio spoke on the VHF.

"Uh Norn," saying the name of our boat wrong, "did you say delta, charlie, 7, 3, 1, alpha, echo, yankee, 6, kilo, foxtrot, delta?"

Pete replied. "Yes, uh roger, just one more alpha after the uh, nancy, on the boat name." I laughed to myself.

Bermuda Radio spoke again, "Norn, please spell the name of your boat."

Pete smiled at me, "Nacho, octopus, rhinoceros, nacho, alligator, over."

"Roger, Norna."

Pete and I were coming into Bermuda at night, nine days after leaving St. Augustine, Florida. We were elated that we had made it, though our legs felt like rubber and we could barely keep our eyes open. The narrow St. George's Channel was calm and opened wide to a bay that bared the same name. We glided Norna up to the concrete wall that was considered the Bermuda Customs dock, after having nervously navigated the reefs and buoys of the entrance. Navigating the area at night was not recommended. Even though the buoys were lit, there were so many marking the reef that they didn't make sense. Bermuda Radio's voice was our guide into this difficult entrance.

We checked in, got our passports stamped, and were told to anchor until morning.

Overwhelmed with sleep, we nonetheless willingly obeyed, fired up the engine and looked for an open spot. The stars mirrored in the dark water. I looked at Norna's reflection, she looked as though she was anchored in the star-scattered sky. We began to relax into the calm rhythm of the night.

As we motored along, to my disappointment, I noticed the engine was smoking. It gave off a faint smell of antifreeze. I remembered our Perkins diesel, which we had nicknamed "The Terrorist," (until we later fixed it and renamed it "Perky") behaving this way once before.

We looked around the anchorage. I quickly shut down the engine and we dropped anchor then and there for the night. We felt comfortable that we were far away from any boats, or land to swing into during tide changes. Pete and I were grateful to smell the flowers and feel the stillness of a calm harbor. We happily laid in bed, and fell asleep.

In my sleep, I heard Bermuda Radio's voice on the VHF.

"This is Bermuda Radio calling Norna, come in Norna." I crawled out of bed and saw it was still night.

"Bermuda Radio, this is Norna?" Half asleep, I waited for a reply.

"Uh, Norna, your running lights are on and you're anchored in the channel."

Bermuda was the first leg of a journey that Pete had dreamed of for a long time. He and I wanted to cross the Atlantic and see blue water sailing, we wanted to see the world! Somehow being out on the blue, our lives and way of thinking began to change. We had somehow, magically, fearfully, amazingly, worked our way out to the water, and the journey wasn't easy.

Chapter Two
The Journey
-St. Augustine, Florida

Journeys by sailboat, much like life itself, rarely go as planned. We had left St. Augustine headed across the Atlantic straight to Ireland, but a torn mainsail led us to Bermuda. The journey— before Pete and Norna— began three years earlier. I was 20 years old.

Back then, before I knew about sailboats, before I had a place of my own, I had my car — a bright yellow Volkswagen beetle, $200 in the bank, my bike, my surfboard, surfboard wax, some summer clothes, pillows, and blankets. I did not have a tent or a way to make shelter. I slept in dark places, away from any houses or people, making a bed in the sand on the beaches near St. Augustine. I came there to find myself and independence, or maybe I wanted to surf and be a bum. I was 21. I knew no one and I had a hard time finding work and meeting people to find roommates. The beach was my shelter.

It was wonderful because I was free; but scary because I was so alone.

I woke up every morning soaking wet as I learned about the dew that fell every night and morning. When it rained, I hid in my yellow car. I showered at an abandoned house that had an outside shower with cold water. I woke up every morning and surfed in the beautiful waves, while watching the pastel swirls of the sunrise. Every night was filled with stars, moon shadows, sand dunes and ghost crabs.

I looked every day for work. I knew of a smoothie place that was being built and was promised a job once the building was completed. I also asked to help with the building, but no one could offer me work. The economy was teetering on the edge of collapse, and workers were being cut back.

I was down to my last $10 for food, and my last meal was bought. I knew that I needed to do something, and I was running out of options. If I could not make it on my own in St. Augustine, I would have to drive back to St. Petersburg on the west coast of Florida, on my last tank of gas, and live with my dad. He had a new house with a new girlfriend, and his own life. It was time for me to move out and make it on my own. I was beginning to feel like a failure.

I walked to a small restaurant that served breakfast and sat down at the table filled with my thoughts and overwhelming loneliness. I had been alone for a month, walking the beach, constantly being disappointed in my search for work, and living out of my car. The only saving grace was that I was close to the water, where I felt so strongly at home, where I could surf. It was the best time of my life, but the scariest because I was alone. I knew no one and was becoming more and more homeless.

The woman who worked in the kitchen looked at me and knew I needed to talk to someone. She asked me my story. I told her that I had a choice between living in a city and going to school every day to become whatever it was I chose to become, or to live on the water, where I was most comfortable. I told her I was down to my last 10 dollars and I was at a crossroads, and

I was not happy with having to drive back to St. Petersburg.

She understood my predicament and told me about a soup kitchen downtown. She cooked me a wonderful breakfast that filled me for most of the day and packed a bean burrito for me to take with me. I was so thankful for someone to talk to and a warm homemade breakfast that I cried back in my car.

Fall was coming and the air was getting colder. Sleeping on the beach and taking cold showers was soon not possible, because it was harder to keep warm. I knew I had to figure something out soon.

The next morning, I drove over the Bridge of Lions into the beautiful town of St. Augustine, with its European architecture and its beautiful waterfront. I couldn't help but look out at the sailboats anchored on the Matanzas River and I took a wrong turn and was lost. I turned onto a brick street with many small stone buildings covered with bougainvillea. I decided it was best to park and ask someone where this soup kitchen was.

I walked along the brick path and felt a warm surge flow through me; I had suddenly realized I was being watched. A man with a thick black beard, round circle sunglasses and a tweed cap was watching me walk. Anxiety crept through me, but I knew I was safe, this man was going to help me.

"You look lost," he said in a Boston accent.

"Yep, you are right. I am. Winter is going to be settling in and I have no warm clothes and no money to buy them. I was looking for the soup kitchen so that I may have something to warm my belly," I answered, slightly ashamed of my predicament, as I knew I was looking homeless.

We were standing outside the mans shop. I looked behind him and saw that there were sewing machines with sails spread out on the floor. I saw there were also several different types of bicycles, some were connected together, and some had lights with mirrors on them. I also saw a fat calico cat sitting in the window, and a young woman measuring a piece of cloth.

"I have a shower in my shop, and I have friends here that have a couch you can stay on until you get your feet on the ground. I also will show you the soup kitchen, hold on one second," he walked into his shop and walked a tricycle out. The tricycle had a low basket before the front wheel that was big enough for a person to sit in.

"Hop in," he told me.

I was reluctant to get in at first. I was unsure of my surroundings and whether I could find my way back to my car. I looked at the man, he seemed kind, although I did not know his name.

"What's your name?" I asked.

"Dylan," he looked at me patiently, "What's yours?"

"Kourtney." I stepped into the basket, and smiled, because I felt like a sack of potatoes being toted around town. Dylan pedaled slow and showed me where his friend's house was. They were my age, wearing mix-matched colorful clothing and their hair was not brushed. They were friendly and told me to come by after I ate.

I was then shown around the back streets and Dylan dropped me off at the soup kitchen. I thanked him. He handed me a jacket I could wear because I was shivering from the cold.

I had never been to a soup kitchen before. I was amazed at the amount of food in the cafeteria. I had assumed there was only soup, but instead there were pastas, breads, vegetables, rice, several kinds of meats, and several choices of desserts and cakes. There were choices of juices or energy drinks, and every person filled their plate to the brim. I was not hungry when I left.

I walked back to my car, slowly following all the backstreets Dylan had shown me, and found that it was not hard to find my way around town. I had energy I had not felt in months. I must have had a smile on my face when I entered Dylan's shop, because he smiled back and asked me if I wanted a shower next. I nodded, and was handed soap and a towel.

I put on clean clothes and the jacket Dylan handed me and walked out into the loft. I saw that Dylan and the friends I had met earlier, were sitting around in a circle smoking a peace pipe. I also noted that the cat was sitting amongst the crowd, as though she was waiting her turn. I joined the circle and smiled again, sitting next to the cat. I was feeling happy and confident that I could figure out what to do with myself.

Dylan asked me if I lived on a boat and I shook my head. I actually didn't know people lived on boats, although I really loved looking out at them and the blue water they floated on. He told me he lived on a sailboat and that I could stop by the next morning if I wanted. He gave me instructions on where to go, while I began to relax. I thanked Dylan for the help and he nodded in agreement. I had realized he had been where I was at some point in his life also. I saw this in many of the people in the soup kitchen; I knew I was not alone.

"There is a bed and breakfast also. My friend here can introduce you to the manager, they are looking for a maid. If you want, you can meet her tomorrow after you stop by my boat," Dylan told me.

I couldn't believe what I was hearing, in a matter of a day; I had stumbled upon one of the nicest strangers, who had a shower, a place for me to stay, and maybe a job? I nodded in disbelief.

"I can't thank you enough Dylan," I said as I left with his friends to stay on their couch for the night. "See you tomorrow."

Chapter Three
Alternative Lifestyle
- St. Augustine, Florida

I woke up the next morning to find that my new friends were awake drinking coffee. I thanked them and asked if I could leave my car at their place. They told me I could stay as long as I wanted, and good luck with the job. I dressed and rode my bike to the bed and breakfast. My friend was there and told me to come in and meet the manager. Soon I was talking about how much I'd be paid and what my hours were going to be. I had a job the next morning to go to.

I walked outside and looked around to see that no one was looking and skipped to my bike. I was going to be able to feed myself again and have money to pay for rent.

I felt like I was floating on my bike as the scenery went by on the way to Dylan's boat. The brick streets soon turned to paved roads again. Trees began to cover the sidewalks, and the uneven roads were soon covered with fallen brown leaves. As I rode further, I saw rundown buildings and abandoned over grown houses. I thought I had understood the instructions Dylan had given me, but I was starting to doubt myself.

I slowed down and was considering turning around, when I heard my name called. I turned and looked to my right and saw a building with a big porch and some people sitting outside playing musical instruments. Dylan was waving to me.

I walked onto the porch, and Dylan introduced me to a man named Dave. He smiled a big silly grin. He had long dreadlocks that went to the middle of his back. He was holding a guitar and wearing overalls. I shook hands with Dave and Dylan explained I was new to town and looking for a place to stay. There was a sign on the porch that said Casa - The Bridge House.

Accidental Sailor Girl

I was shown around. The house had several rooms upstairs with friends who were living there. Some rooms were empty, but had beds or dressers, and there were multiple showers. There was a large kitchen downstairs with two stoves and fridges, and a back porch with a washer and dryer that I was told I could use. Dave told me to stop by and hang out.

Dave had also told me that he worked for Dylan in his sail loft, and Dylan was getting ready to move back to Boston in a few weeks. Dave told me he found another job with a local boat carpenter named Pete, and asked me if I wanted to stay in the hostel. I did not realize that Casa - The Bridge House, was a hostel. I told him I might, because I didn't want to couch surf for too long and wear out my welcome. He asked me if I played music, which I did not at the time. I stayed and listened until it became dusk.

After listening to Dave play, Dylan told me to follow him to the boat. I noticed it was right around the corner. I parked my bicycle and walked out onto the wooden dock. The boat was tied so that Dylan pulled in a rope to swing the boat closer to step onto. I followed his lead, and stepped aboard.

We climbed the ladder to go below and I was awed by the musty smell and warmness of the dark cabin. I slowly worked my way to the companionway and could see light through the circle portholes in the side of the cabin house. One port was open and the cat from the sail loft wiggled its way inside, and pounced onto the seat I was walking toward. Dylan set his bags down and lit his oil lamps with a match. Light filled the cabin as they glowed and cast shadows onto the wooden table. The cat was purring loudly and cleaning its paws. I sat next to it.

Dylan grabbed a glass and poured a drink into it, he handed it to me. I told him I had quit drinking. He nodded and pulled out chocolate soy milk and handed me a glass. He sat down, his cat looked up from its cleaning. It felt awkward in the silence, but I had many questions to ask. I did not know which ones to ask, because I knew nothing of boats.

I began by asking him if he lived aboard full time. He nodded, and said that he was going to move his sail loft to Boston and fly back down to Florida to move the boat up. I asked him if he needed help moving his sail loft, and if he did, I would be more than willing to help him move. I asked him what kind was the right boat, where to find boats, how to anchor them, and how to know how to work on them. I never thought that people might live aboard their boats. My dad had a boat when I was growing up. We use to take it to islands on the Gulf and spend the day, or a few nights camping out, but living on a boat had never crossed my mind.

I was so excited to learn about this alternative lifestyle. I wanted to live on the water and have a roof over my head, but I knew I could not afford rent on the water. I was surprised to learn that sailors could anchor for free in most harbors that allowed this, and I was ready to start looking for a sailboat as soon as I could.

Dylan helped me outside. He wished me luck on my new job in the morning. He also noted that if I wanted to stop by his sail loft and help him move in the afternoon, after I got off of work, that that would be great. I agreed and hugged his cat goodnight.

I woke from my couch and went to work the next morning. That evening, I helped Dylan move. Dave was also at the sail loft helping, and he showed me what went in which box. This continued for a few days as Dave and I became friends. I would meet him later at the Hostel and listen to him play music.

Dave and I said our goodbyes to Dylan and I thanked him for all his help and patience with me. I was grateful he had found me places to stay, a job that could pay me, and a new path to take in finding a place to live that I could afford. I had finally found what I came to St. Augustine for!

Chapter Four

The Unveiling
-St. Augustine & St. Petersburg, Florida

Weeks went by, and I couch surfed from place to place, as I worked at the bed and breakfast. Dave, and the many friends at the hostel house lent me warm friendships, and a nice place to stop by and relax for the evenings. I could cook meals on their stoves, and sleep in one of their rooms for the night if I needed to.

I walked on the docks, or the waterfront every day, and looked out at the sailboats. I wondered how I would find a place on the water too. I saw a few boats for sale. Many were sinking, or gutted, or missing masts. I knew I was going to live on a boat someday, I just didn't know if I would find the right one in St. Augustine.

I visited my dad for Christmas that year. I had a vacation from the bed and breakfast, and my dad paid for my gas to drive over to St. Petersburg. He wanted to see me and make sure I was OK, and if I had found a place to rent. I had not, because I was in search of a boat.

Accidental Sailor Girl

I arrived in St. Petersburg after a four-hour drive, and gave my dad and stepmom a hug. I was shown my room. I unpacked my things, showered, and dressed for dinner in an hour. I looked at my clothes and the small amount of things I owned, and looked around the room of my dad's house. It was filled with decorations, furniture, carpet, and a closet. I laughed to myself of how different I had become.

We sat to dinner. My dad asked me how I was doing and if I had found a place to live and work yet. I told him I had found work, and that I had not yet found a rental because I had a different plan.

"Dad, I am going to get a sailboat." My dad became silent, he looked disappointed with my decision. My dad worked more than 30 years on the police force during this time (though he later retired in 2011). After dinner, he took me in a patrol car and brought me underneath a bridge in a rather poor part of St. Petersburg. There were empty beer cans, tin cans, torn mattresses, and a fire pit. Homeless people had obviously lived in this place. My dad looked at me with concern. "These people are going to get a sailboat too."

Chapter Five
Homeless No More
-St. Augustine, Florida

I was determined to show my dad I could make it on my own. I desperately wanted to be independent. I drove back to St. Augustine on a mission—I was going to find a sailboat, no matter what.

I returned back to the brick street where I first met Dylan and his cat, and I followed the back streets he had shown me so carefully before. I walked with my thoughts bundled in my pocket ready to explode out onto the road as a ball of fire. I walked past the Bridge House and did not see Dave or anyone home. I continued to the dock, where I had first boarded a sailboat. I walked out onto its wooden planks and looked out to the river at the egrets standing in the mudflats preening their feathers. I walked down to Dylan's boat and looked at it. Dylan was going to return for his boat and take it to Boston at some point. I wondered when he would return, or if he ever would. I then heard a man behind me.

"He is not there."

I turned around. There was a tall skinny man with the smell of liquor on his breath. His face had long signs of use and his skin was like leather. He wore torn jeans splattered with paint and he had a drunken smile that hid his eyes in wrinkles. I thought of Popeye.

I smiled back, "I know, I was looking at his boat to get an idea as to what kind of sailboat I want to buy."

The man nodded and smiled again, "I have a sailboat for sale right behind ya."

I turned around and there it was. As though another piece of magic had unrolled itself forward in time. I walked closer. I did not know the kind of boat but I knew three things: the boat had to have a clean title, had to have a diesel inboard engine, and had to be floating. I saw the boat *was* floating and that it had a mast with sails. It was around the same size as Dylan's boat.

I looked at the man, "Can I have a look inside?"

The man walked over with me, climbed aboard and opened the hatches. I walked below and saw that it was really moldy, there were foam cushions without covers on them. There was a small alcohol stove and a sink. I asked the man his name.

"Jeremy," he said, he then asked me mine and showed me the diesel engine. It was a Yanmar engine. He explained that the title was free and clear and that it was for sale for $4,000.

I told him I would have to pay it off, because I did not have that much saved.

"You can move on it today if you want. Pay me each month $150, and work out the rent for the dockage with the dock master," Jeremy offered.

I agreed and we wrote a contract. Jeremy told me he would give me the title when the boat was paid for.

I was homeless no more! I moved in that day, cleaned and bleached. I found cushion covers to fit the foam and made my bed. I found alcohol to put in the stove and cooked my first meal on the boat. Spaghetti.

I wanted to learn everything there was to know about my boat. It was the first boat I had ever owned. It was a 1977, 27-foot Hunter. I later learned that Jeremy was lucky to have sold the boat as it was in miserable condition. I was so happy to find a home and a purpose that I appreciated every bit of it. It had a nice layout inside. There was an open galley and companionway, a walkthrough head with no toilet installed, and a forward V-bunk. I was told it was a good Bahamas boat, and I wanted to learn everything I could to fix it up.

I lived aboard at the dock, working to pay off the boat, until my dad gave me a nice cushion of $4,000. This was inheritance money from the death of my mother when I was 14. I was originally meant to use this money for college.

I payed off the boat and started a new life in my new home. Jeremy gave me the title to my sailboat, which I named "Happy." Happy had a Yanmar diesel engine, which needed a new water pump, all the sails, a caving-in cabin top, a clean title, a dirty bottom, and a good spirit.

Chapter Six
Row Row Row Your Boat
-St. Augustine, Florida

I lived aboard Happy on the dock for five months, before paying off the boat. I had made more friends, and started working at a new place called Sailors Exchange. The weather was warming, summer was returning, and I knew I wanted to move off the dock and anchor out on the harbor.

As I was considering anchoring and learning about what kind of ground tackle I needed, I met a man named Scottie at Sailors Exchange. He talked loosely and looked like a grey wizard. He had a long grey pointy beard, long grey hair, and circle glasses. His clothes were torn with patches and paint, and he looked to be about 70. He asked me why I was working at Sailors Exchange. I told him I was working to buy parts for my boat, though I did not know what most of the parts were. He told me to meet him on the wall of the Matanzas River, where I saw the many boats anchored, because he had some work for me. I gladly took in work. I wanted to know everything I could learn about boats, and as I worked at Sailors Exchange, I never stopped asking "What's this for?"

I met Scottie after my shift. To my surprise he was rowing a small double-ended dinghy to pick me up and take me out to his boat. I knew there were boats out on the bay, as I would stare at them daily, but I never stopped to think how people got to them.

I walked in wonder to his dinghy and sat down inside.

He snickered a little and told me to get out because he had to push it back into the water to float! I watched as he dragged the little dingy along the mud into the water. I saw that his clothes were wet, and he was mostly muddy from the attempt, but he looked pleased with himself and told me to take a seat. I rolled up my pants legs and sat in the now-floating dingy.

He was quiet on the row to the boat. I felt somewhat uncomfortable, seeing as I didn't know the man, and he looked a little crazy. The row seemed like forever, but Scottie rowed confidently and we made it to his boat, a red sailboat, with a funny smell coming out of the cockpit.

Scottie haphazardly tied his dingy off to a lifeline, as he had done thousands of times before, and told me to climb above the lifelines. I listened very well and climbed under, and must have looked strange trying to squeeze my body through.

We were boarded and I watched as his dingy floated back, stopping abruptly at the knot on the lifeline. The boat rocked, and the breeze was cold on the water. I looked back to the land; it was a completely different point of view. I looked down at the water. Scottie suggested I go down below with him, but I opted to stay in the cockpit. I felt apprehensive of what kind of work this man was offering.

He lit his alcohol stove and placed a clay pot on top to warm the cabin.

"It's nice and warm on land," I said.

Scottie looked at me over his glasses, "Yeah, you sure you don't want to come down below?"

I shook my head no.

"Fine, stay outside, here's a wrench," he said.

I looked at the wrench as if it was an alien invader and I was the poor little children's toy it was going to zap.

I watched as Scottie popped open a beer with his screwdriver, "want a beer?"

"No thanks, I quit."

He looked at me again over his glasses, "OK, hold this nut."

He pointed to a nut on the cabin house. I was still in shock that I was on a boat with a man I didn't know, in a harbor I knew nothing about; with no way ashore except to swim.

He almost laughed at my face; I think he understood I was naive. I held the nut, sort of, not understanding what he was doing underneath. I tried my best to do as I was told, and I guessed I did OK, because Scottie called me "grunge", and told me I was crazy.

It was time to go, and we boarded his dinghy. He told me to meet him on the wall of the Matanzas River the next day after my shift.

In my total bewilderment, I met him on the wall the next day. I sat in his dinghy, the right way this time, except, I guessed the wrong spot, because he gave me his oars, and told me to row.

So, I rowed, I think, or not. I was going in circles. I hit my knee. I ended up back at the wall. Scottie laughed at my accomplishment, and took the oars to show me how to pull the oars toward me in one fluid movement, and to look at a certain point to row in that direction.

I took the oars back and decided on a streetlight on the road. I rowed, the wrong way, in circles, pushed back to find that streetlight. I somehow found the movement, but lost it again, and within 15 strokes, Scottie took the oars and rowed the rest of the way.

I don't remember what he said at that moment, but I knew he had taken that moment in as the memory of his first time he had rowed a boat. He wasn't too hard on me, just called me a few names.

My friendship with Scottie was a sweet introduction of how to live in a harbor on a sailboat. I wanted to live in the beautiful harbor too, and move from the dock. I was missing the ocean, and its sounds, and the refreshment it brought when I swam.

My engine was not working. I had bought two sets of anchors, chain and rope. What I needed next was a dinghy, and a way to get out to the anchorage.

I heard through people at work that Scottie was selling that little double-ended dingy he had shown me how to row on, for $300. I waited for Scottie to show up at Sailors Exchange and offer me more work, but he did not show up that day. I wanted to talk to him about the dinghy. After my shift, I rode my bike down to the waterfront.

The dinghy was anchored off the seawall and floating, which meant Scottie was on shore somewhere. I picked a bottle out of a nearby trashcan and found a piece of paper and a pen in my backpack. I scribbled a note that said that I would have $300 for him tomorrow after work and the time I would be on the wall, and rolled the note into the bottle. I stood on the wall looking into the dinghy and hoped that I had good aim to toss the bottle into his little boat. I counted to three, and astonishingly it landed with a thud on a pile of rope, in plain view for Scottie to see.

The next day, after I got off of work, I quickly rode my bike down to the seawall. The dinghy was gone. I looked out to his red boat at anchor and saw that it was safely tied alongside.

I called to him, but realized that it was no use wasting my voice. I patiently sat on the seawall. I sat there for three hours staring at the red boat and his little dingy with $300 in my hand. I stared at his boat, and was determined to sit on the wall all night if I had to. Finally, I saw him rowing toward shore.

He came to the seawall, saw me sitting, and gave me a quizzical look. I wondered if he had gotten my note.

I asked him about the sale. "No" he said.

I felt so conquered. I needed to find another dingy, and I didn't know where to look. Scottie saw my disappointment, and he thought about it for a second.

"Get in the dingy, you should practice rowing."

Scottie dropped the dinghy off – of which I later named Bipolar - the next day after the sale. He next showed me how to splice an anchor line. He told me to be ready in the morning. He was going to help me get off the dock. I thanked him, and thanked my stars that I was off work the next day to be able to do so.

I spliced the remainder of my line and I tied my anchors off to the bow of my boat. I tied the dinghy to the side of Happy and I made ready for

the change in scenery I would have the next
morning. I went to visit Dave at the Hostel house
and I spent the remainder of the night having a
celebratory dinner.

The next morning came quickly and I was
groggy from being awoken early from a knock on
my hull. It took me a long time to wake up.
Scottie then starting rocking my boat back and
forth to roll me out of bed. I sleepily stuck my
head outside. I was not ready to leave the dock; I
was becoming nervous about moving my boat.
Scottie starting untying my dock lines. I
became more awake. I jumped out into the
cockpit and exclaimed that I was nervous about
moving my boat. I didn't have a working engine.
Scottie handed me a boat pole, and got in the
dingy. He tied the dingy to the front of the boat
and explained to me that I needed to move now,
because the tide was right to move. He began
rowing my boat forward and he explained to me
that I needed to fend off with a boat pole.
We passed one docked boat without
incident, and then the next. We soon were out
into the channel, into the strong current. Scottie
rowed Happy across the current, out of the
channel, and told me to drop my first anchor. I
did as I was told. He asked me if I had it tied, and
I did.

"Now, let the boat fall back, and you will feel it catch on the anchor. Once it turns into the stream and stops, tug on the anchor line and let the anchor grab." Scottie explained.

I did as I was told and we were successfully anchored. He untied the dingy from the front of the boat and rowed to my side, tied off, and climbed aboard.

"Good job, now we wait a little while and I will row a second anchor behind you so that when you swing in the tide, your boat will stay where it is." Scottie explained, "This is called Bahamian moor."

I put away extra dock lines and double-checked everything was cleated off. Scottie rowed the next anchor out and set it to the opposite angle.

I looked out to my old dock place. I saw Dylan's boat floating in its slip, and I smiled to myself because I was actually anchored out. I was amazed at how much I was learning. It was a whole different feeling being away from shore, even though I was a few feet away.

Scottie sat down in the cockpit of my boat after finishing setting the second anchor, "I am going to get some friends to help move you to the anchorage, out on the harbor, in the next couple days."

I nodded.

Scottie watched, amused, as I untangled line from the mess of anchor rode, "I want you to stay here a few days, and practice rowing."

Chapter Seven
A Tourist Attraction
-St. Augustine, Florida

I was towed by Scottie's friends in front of the Castillo de San Marcos fort, in the beautiful harbor of St. Augustine. I felt a weight lifted off my chest. I had successfully moved from a dock. I was now out on the blue water that I dreamed about every day. I was among the boats. Instead of looking out at them, I was a part of them.

I had started to gain calluses and muscles from rowing. I learned to time winds and tides because of the current that ripped through the Matanzas River. This current would take a sailor out the inlet, and out to sea, without a fight.

I started to learn the difficulties of living on the water, possibilities I hadn't even thought of. Going to and from my boat was hard, much less carrying food. I did not have running water or a fridge, and my solar panel gave the batteries enough juice to power my lights for a few hours at night. I would haul heavy water jugs, and the constant change in weather was always a challenge.

I was given a cat by a friend. She was a very large cat. Her belly touched the ground, and she was striped like a grey tiger. She had a bad attitude, and would attack if I held her. I named her Doodles. It was always a challenge to find a place for her litter box on my small boat. She seemed to feel at home on Happy as much as I did. She would curiously poke her head over the edge to look at the fish below.

One morning, I took Doodles for a row in Bipolar. The wind was blowing steady and the sky was threatening to rain. As I was rowing ashore, I saw that Doodles was sniffing an umbrella I brought. She looked at me curiously. I opened it to show her what it was, and discovered that I could sail right up onto the beach. This was too much fun. I pushed off the beach and sailed back to Happy. Wow! I was sailing my umbrella in my little double-ended dinghy with my cat Doodles. I turned around again to sail back to shore, feeling like a kid again. I continued doing so until my stomach growled for food. I sailed up to Happy as close as I could, grabbed the oars, and rowed the rest of the way.

The fort in St. Augustine was called Castillo De San Marco. It was built by the Spanish and the river was named Matanzas or *massacre,* from the numerous battles and the bloodshed at the Matanzas Inlet. The water had supposedly turned the color of blood.

The fort was a National Park and was protected, so dinghies were not allowed to tie up to its walls. If a sailor did tie up, he would be ticketed, and his dinghy would be removed.

I learned from Scottie that the best way to circumvent this issue was to anchor the dinghy away from the wall. Scottie would row up to the seawall and climb the stairs with the dingy anchor in his hand. The dinghy would be floating in the water below, tied to this anchor. He would then throw the anchor out into the water. His dinghy would obey, and float away from the prohibited wall. I learned how much line was needed to safely anchor my dinghy for tide changes, as well.

Next, Scottie showed me a flat piece of wood with line wrapped around it. At the end of the line was a grappling hook. This hook and line, I learned, was a system to retrieve the anchored dinghy. Scottie would unravel the line and stand on the piece of wood. He then would throw the hook, aiming for the anchor line attached to the dinghy. Sometimes it would take a few tries, but once the line was captured, the whole system was retrieved with the anchor line attached. The dinghy could then be pulled in close, in order to climb inside and row away. This technique served me well during the times I was anchored in front of the fort. It made life much easier, and helped to transport food and water.

I became a tourist attraction on the wall of the fort, as people would walk up and ask me about my story. It was fun to talk to the many people who were fascinated with the fact that a young girl was living out on her own boat, by herself. Many people would stand behind me and watch me retrieve the dinghy. Sometimes a person would ask if they could try to throw the grappling hook and catch the anchor line themselves.

Chapter Eight

Careening
-St. Augustine, Florida

I knew that the bottom of my boat needed to be examined and painted. I had never seen the bottom, and I was nervous as to its condition. I knew when I bought Happy that the bottom had a live coral reef on its bottom. The many friends I had made in the anchorage offered to help me careen her. I could not afford to haul her out. I was more afraid of hauling out and paying bills than I was of beaching Happy and painting her myself.

There was a little shoaling island north of the Castillo de San Marcos fort that appeared at low tide that everyone at the anchorage called Bird Island. Behind this island was a soft spot that was away from waves. It was mostly invisible to people and I knew I could spend two days painting Happy.

I was towed to this place, and dropped an anchor in the middle of the channel. I then was instructed to hang an anchor off my boom. and to bring this anchor to land. This ensured that my boat would lean the right way toward shore. Everyone was worried whether my boat would right itself when the tide rose. As the tide began to drop, I positioned Happy to lie over on her starboard side using the anchor. I then moved all of my things to the low side of the boat and prepared for painting, by bringing materials to the beach.

Slowly, the tide began to drop, and Happy laid over farther and farther until the water was completely gone from the keel. As the tide dropped, I could stand on land where the water had been. I began to scrape off barnacles and stir paint. I knew I had six hours until full high tide returned.

I successfully got paint onto Happy with the help of my friends from the anchorage, and made ready for the tide to turn. I prepared for either a sunk, or a floating boat. I decided it would be best to stay on the beach with my dinghy until Happy floated, so I made camp with Doodles. I looked inside Happy and felt my head spin, as the cabin was dizzyingly turned the wrong way. Doodles decided to jump inside. As she pounced on the stairs, I heard a clanging of pots and pans. She had realized that the boat was not at the same angle she was used to anymore. I decided to rescue her, and climbed the seats and the walls to grab her and throw her back into the cockpit.

That night, I walked the small beach alone, and looked at the stars. I sat on the cold sand and watched Happy. The tide was starting to come up the sides of her hull and she looked to be starting to float. She was safely bobbing up and down on her side.

I suddenly heard a faint sort of "Meowma."

I looked around on the beach, I knew Doodles was prowling around, and I worried she was in trouble.

"DOODLES!?" I yelled as I wandered the small beach. The tide was coming in and I knew some parts of the beach would disappear.

"Meowma!" It sounded as though she was saying "momma." I walked toward the sound and found her crunched up in a ball holding something in her paws. I kneeled down.

"What is it Doodles, what do you have?" Doodles had a sort of smile on her face and her tail was wagging like a dog's. She opened her paws and there appeared a small, scared ghost crab. It looked up at me and appeared unharmed, and as soon as it was free, it skidded its sideways dance into a hole.

I looked over at Happy and saw that she was happily floating at her anchor. She was ready to be turned the other way for the next tide drop the following day. I rowed out that night knowing my boat could right itself, this was a nice feeling indeed.

I soon was back in the anchorage with a clean and painted bottom, and with confidence to careen her again.

Chapter Nine
Bluegrass Pete
-St. Augustine, Florida

I was becoming lonely anchored out alone on my sailboat. I would row to shore just to ride my bike around and talk to people. I would wander around the backstreets of St. Augustine and listen to the local music whenever I walked past.

One night, I was riding my bike through an area that I had not visited before, and I saw Dave playing music at a bar. I stopped and stood in the doorway to watch, and once the band had taken a break, Dave came over and introduced me to his friend Pete. Pete had shaggy brown hair, an unkempt beard, and was wearing a ball cap. His eyes were friendly and he smiled warmly. He had a country accent that gave him a sort of sweet disposition, and he held a guitar in his arms.

I shook his hand and talked with him a bit as Dave went to get a drink. Pete told me he heard I lived on a boat and told me he lived on a sailboat too. He explained that his boat was hauled out at the moment, as he was doing the copper bottom. I didn't ask anymore questions because I did not know what a copper bottom was.

Dave returned with his drink and a few other friends. Dave told me that Pete and his band were going to be playing at Pete's wood shop after dinner the following night and to stop by. He told me that it was right down the road from Dylan's marina and that Pete was the woodworker he had started working for. I accepted the invitation and started to worry about my little dinghy. I often worried about my dinghy anchored out. I would return to it several times a day to make sure it was not stolen. I said my goodbyes, and rode off into the night.

I rode to the seawall of the fort and saw my dinghy was where I had left it. I unraveled my grappling hook, and as I was beginning to toss it into the water to fetch my anchor, I heard my name called. I looked behind me and saw Pete drive by on his way home.

The next evening, I walked over to Pete's woodworking shop to watch Dave and Pete play with their band. On my way inside, I saw a wooden sailboat that looked like a small ship of about 40 feet parked outside, and many boat molds. The shop was an old tin scallop house on the river. Behind it, shrimp boats were docked with their many nets laid out on the lot. Their bright spotlights shone on their long outriggers. It made them look like strange crab-like ships.

Accidental Sailor Girl

I walked inside Pete's shop and was immediately immersed in the sound of bluegrass music. I looked around. Pete and Dave were playing with a banjo player, and standing in a circle around a single microphone. I saw planers and chop boxes, skill saws, many rusty hand tools lying about, and about seven surfboards stacked next to an old dusty fridge. I was approached by some friends of Pete's. They were enjoying listening as much as I was.

I sat on the table saw and was approached by a very strange-looking dog. It was medium sized, had large pointy ears and was slim and muscular. Its short stubby tail was wagging its entire bottom half and it had white teeth that took up its entire long snout. Its eyes were small and dark, complete with small eyelashes, that somehow made the whole gremlin of a dog, look friendly. I looked at the complete shape of the animal, and as I was analyzing it, I heard Pete say, "Wanna meet my puppy?"

I looked at Pete and to my surprise blurted, "That's not a puppy, it's an alien!"

Pete laughed at my exclamation and then warmly asked how my boat was doing. I began to blush. Was this man really making my stomach do flips? I shook off my feelings.

"I am having problems with the rooftop leaking, I think I may have a rotten cabin top as I heard that it was a balsa core," and as I was talking, I looked at Pete and saw that he looked to be around 35. I wasn't sure, but I knew he was an older man. Oh no, did I have a crush on him?

"I can stop out tomorrow if you want and take a look at it," Pete said, as he tried to calm the hyper dog down. It had stood on its hind legs and was sniffing around for any food on tables.

I thought about the date and realized it was a Sunday. I had made plans that morning, to drop my mast with the help of a man named Steve and his friend Mike, who both had Cheoy Lee sailboats.

"I really do need the help right now, I would really appreciate it," I said.

Dave came over and gave me a hug. The dog came with him and was wagging its tail at him the same way.

"What's your dog's name, Pete?" I petted the black beast.

"Leelo, she is a medium-sized mutt. She makes a really good boat dog because she doesn't have a tail to hit you in the face and bang up the boat." Pete set his guitar down.

"I am putting my boat in the water tomorrow. We are finally done coppering the bottom. I am going to make a mooring out in Salt

Run and anchor out there. I can take my dinghy around the corner and meet you tomorrow on your boat around two o'clock?" Pete asked me.

I nodded. I asked him where Salt Run was. He explained to me that if I was coming from St. Augustine inlet, I would make an immediate left. He explained to me about a Spanish Watchtower that was built in the 1500's that had been built near an old inlet. It later had been destroyed by a storm. The new lighthouse, built in 1824 (called the St. Augustine Lighthouse) was built on Anastasia Island.

I spent the rest of the night talking and listening to music. I decided it best to leave as my worry for my dinghy began to creep on me, and the wind had picked up. I rode my bike to the wall, fetched my dinghy, and made ready for the busy morning ahead.

Chapter Ten
Falling Masts
-St. Augustine, Florida

The next morning came. I knew I was going to have a busy morning. My friends were going to help me drop my mast, and Pete was arriving to meet me later that day.

I sat on the bow of my sailboat in the harbor and watched as the tide started to drop. The fish began jumping around the rocks of the fort. I watched the sunrise, as I fed Doodles her breakfast. I looked around the anchorage. I was anchored with two sets of ground tackle (Bahamian moor). I positioned Happy in front of the fort. I could angle my row with the tides, as the water would rush in or out of the inlet just behind me.

Beside me, about 20 feet away, was a black Cheoy Lee sailboat. It was starting to turn its bow into the stream of current. Two boats down, toward the Bridge of Lions was another Cheoy Lee sailboat, and it too, was beginning to turn. I watched as simultaneously the two boats started to rock, and then just as orderly, the two gentlemen that were to help me with my mast, were standing on deck with their cups of coffee. I laughed to myself as I waved to them. I knew that in another hour, they would both fire up their engines, and move their boats on either side of mine. We had talked about this a few days previously.

I prepared the saw horses on my deck where I was to lay my mast, and I started to remove cotter pins on the turnbuckles. While I was undoing my last turnbuckle, I saw that Steve and Mike were pulling up their anchors. Steve was first to approach. I tied even amounts of fenders on both sides of my boat and prepared to catch Steve's line to tie to Happy. He pulled alongside. I tied his bow line to a cleat on my bow, and Steve jumped aboard and tied his stern. Next was Mike. He pulled to the other side of Happy, and I helped tie Mike off.

They explained that they were going to use their mast halyards to hold my mast from falling down. They began to tie line around it, and I started to undo the turnbuckles. We were surprised to find that the mast was not pulling off its boot, after the last turnbuckle was undone. We tugged, and nothing was working.

Steve decided that I would have to use a sawzall to cut through the bolts on the boot that went thru the deck of the coach roof. I was beginning to fade from hunger. I agreed that the best thing to do, was for me to row to the other side of the bay, two miles away, and ask a friend if I could borrow a battery operated sawzall.

My hands were blistered and I was famished. I rowed four miles, and returned to my boat with the saw that was to cut my mast free. I took a break and ate lunch. Steve and Mike were determined to get my mast free, and I couldn't be more thankful.

We made ready and cut through the mast-step bolts with a fight. As soon as the last bolt broke, the mast fell. The lines from Steve's and Mike's boat were doing their job, but the weight of my mast, and the tugging and straining of the two boats rubbing on my boat's side, was becoming a precarious situation. The current was already full force. It was putting a working on my anchors with two boats tied alongside.

I looked around to be sure I was not dragging with the whole lot attached. I saw that I was still placed next to the fort in the alignment for me to row in and out.

Steve and Mike lowered my mast onto the saw horses and we made ready to untie Mike's boat. Steve watched as Mike safely motored off and he next jumped on his boat, turned on his motor, and motored away.

I stood by my mast and looked around the harbor. I saw that a crowd had formed on the walls of the fort and that there were people pointing at my boat. I looked around, but I was still anchored safely. I watched as my two friends safely anchored in the same places a few feet away, and began to tie my mast to its saw horses.

I turned on my VHF radio, and I heard Steve and Mike talking to each other. I listened for a while, and realized they were talking about a hurricane, called Fay, that was coming our way in a few days. They were worried for me. They talked about what their plans were. Steve mentioned he would be willing to tow me to a dock, but that I needed to get my engine working soon, or I would be in trouble.

I began to worry. I was unaware of the tropical storm coming to St. Augustine, and I was not prepared. I was anchored dangerously close to the fort and the waves from the ocean could come right into the inlet, if the storm was big. I did not want to risk being anchored out during a hurricane with my mast on saw horses and no way to move without an engine. I had two days to prepare!

Chapter Eleven

Happy Moves
 -St. Augustine, Florida

I tied my mast down to its saw horses as tightly as I could to my deck and as I was in the middle of putting away cotter pins and rigging wires, I saw a boat that looked like a coconut coming closer to Happy. Doodles ran up on deck. She had hidden down below from the commotion of the sawzall and the two boats tied alongside.

I squinted, and saw a black dog with pointy ears standing tall on the bow of a coconut shaped dinghy. It was balancing with all four paws on the thin strip of cap rail, while the dinghy bounced through waves. As the coconut came closer, I saw a man in a white shirt standing and steering a little white two horse engine in the back. I realized it was Pete and his dog Leelo. The coconut dinghy was a wooden (mahogany) 12 foot boat. It had a duck bill bow that displaced the water to either side and had a dry interior because of this. I waved to Pete, and Leelo began to bark. Doodles wagged her tail like a dog, and I stood in my cockpit in amusement.

Pete pulled alongside and Leelo curiously sniffed over the bow, as Doodles approached her. They both looked at each other and began wagging their tails.

"I heard there was a tropical storm named Fay coming, and I thought I would come a little sooner than two," Pete smiled up at me.

"Please come aboard," I said, "I have just dropped my mast with the help of two Cheoy Lees."

Pete climbed aboard and motioned if Leelo could come aboard also. I nodded. Pete walked up to my cabin top and stepped around where the old mast step once resided.

"Yeah, it is really spongy Kourtney," Pete looked at me with concern.

Leelo began to bark at Doodles, as Doodles hissed back. Pete held Leelo and started to put her back in the coconut dinghy.

"I think they will get along," I said, "Just give them a minute to get used to each other's company."

Pete let go and the black alien dog shot after Doodles like a rocket. Doodles ran below.

We both laughed as Leelo ran after her. She was stopped short as the door to the companionway was closed enough for only Doodles to fit.

"I don't have a working engine," I proceeded to tell Pete, "I have tried everything I've learned. I have opened each injector to clear the lines of air, cleaned out the fuel, and checked all electrical connections."

Pete walked to the companionway, and I opened the doors to invite him below.

"The engine is underneath the stairs," I said to Pete, as he pulled the stairs up to take a look. He looked at my little Yanmar engine and followed a hose that went to the through-hull fitting in the bottom of my boat. It had duck tape and a cork stuck in it. He looked at me.

"This hose is the seawater intake," he said. "What happened to the through-hull?"

I explained to him how it was a faucet knob from a house, instead of a seacock valve, that corroded and broke. I tried to turn it on, and when it broke, water rushed in— I used the cork and duct tape. He pointed to a through-hull beside it that had a correct valve.

"Is this the seacock to your sink?"

He followed a hose and found it to be from the drain of my sink. He closed the valve, and undid the sink hose attached to it. He next attached the line for the seawater intake of the engine to the working valve and turned it open.

I watched him double-check the engine. Pete looked up at me and asked me to turn it over. I turned the engine key and it started right away. He asked me to put the engine in forward gear, and Happy began to push forward. I was next told to put the engine in neutral. Again, I was asked to put the engine in reverse. I did so, and the boat began to tug on its anchors backwards. I put it back in neutral. My engine was finally working!

Pete put the stairs back together, and the putt-putt of the little Yanmar continued to smoothly run.

"You are really lucky your motor did not start without water running through it, you could have burned out your pump and impeller." Pete walked up to the bow to look at my anchor situation.

"I can put you behind my shop to repair the cabin top if you want, it should be safe back there from the tropical storm, because it is behind buildings. It should be sheltered." Pete walked back to his dinghy to tie it off farther astern, "are you ready to move?"

I looked at him with what must have been shock. I was not ready, but what could I say to this handsome, bearded man? That I don't know how to drive a boat with a motor, I had been towed around all this time? That I didn't know if I had enough diesel fuel, that I was really nervous to move from my spot I had been for half a year? I felt vulnerable.

"I don't know if I have enough diesel fuel," I said doubtfully.

Pete looked at his phone for the time, "The bridge opens every half hour. We have about 15 minutes before the next opening, just enough time to get your anchors pulled. We can fuel up at the St. Augustine Marina, just on the other side of the bridge." He looked toward the Bridge of Lions, "It is an easy dock to pull up to," he added.

Pete and I pulled up Happy's anchors and Pete gave me the wheel to steer. The Bridge of

Lions opened on time and I slowly motored through. Thoughts were overwhelming me. I had never docked a boat before. I had docked my dinghy Bipolar, but that was under my own power. It wasn't 27 feet long. I looked over to Pete as we approached the St. Augustine Marina's fuel dock, and he knew by my facial expressions, that I was unsure of what to do.

"You are with the current. When you pull up on the starboard side, put yourself in forward and then neutral. Once you get closer, put the engine in reverse, and then neutral, and you will slowly pull in."

I did as I was told, and to my surprise Happy was docked, and I was fueling up. We untied the lines from the dock and were off to Pete's shop. On the way, I remembered the night I had walked over to watch Pete play music in his shop. I thought of the docks behind where the shrimp boaters docked to refuel and unload their catch. This was where we were motoring to. I was really glad that I was putting Happy somewhere safe for the storm, and that I had help to fix her caving-in cabin top.

We entered the San Sabastion River and looked to a tight empty slip between two shrimp boats. I could see the tin scallop buildings on land a few feet away. Pete again told me what to do and I slowly eased into the dock. He then tied me off safely. I was so glad to have made it to a dock, that I had forgotten Doodles was on board. She sprinted out of the cabin and onto solid ground. Pete grabbed Leelo to stop her from following.

"She will run away." He clipped Leelo's leash on. "The first time my daughter Ava and I had gotten Leelo from the pound, she ran away. I tried to put her in the back of my truck, but she would block the entrance with her legs. She somehow had squirmed away and ran off across the street. Next thing we knew, we were running after this black dog through a cemetery. Not only were we running after her through a cemetery, but there was a funeral being held. Leelo ran right through it! She ran right through the bagpipers' legs! Ava, my daughter, eventually caught her."

I laughed, "Doodles will come when she is called," I said, "She knows where her bread is buttered."

So Pete had a daughter, I didn't stop myself from asking questions, "So where is Ava now? Is she at your shop?"

Pete looked at me, I expected to see surprise, but was glad to see that I did not offend him, "Ava is with her mom in Flagler. We divorced about two years ago. She didn't want to live on the boat anymore, I don't blame her."

He smiled. I couldn't help but want to ask more questions, but I decided it best to keep it business.

"So, I remember you telling me you were going to put your boat in the water, did you get anchored in Salt Run?" I smiled back.

"Yes, actually, I was going to head out there and put my third anchor down. I am making a mooring, hopefully it holds for the tropical storm coming in a couple days."

I looked at Happy, and at Doodles. She looked content to finally have her paws on land.

"Do you need help? I think Happy will be fine here, and Doodles knows where her food is, no one will steal anything, will they?"

"No, it usually takes thieves a few days to notice," Pete untied his dinghy, and pulled it alongside on the last amount of dock space.

"That would be great if you could help. Secure your dinghy, I will pull my dingy out of the water, and pull my car down to put it in the back."

Chapter Twelve

Norna
-St. Augustine, Florida

Pete's coconut dinghy was surprisingly light. The little two-horse outboard on the back made the backside a little heavier. Pete had a heck of a time pulling it onto the dock, but we safely had the dinghy inside the truck and were on our way to Salt Run.

"I will dive on that seacock tomorrow and repair it before the storm for you," Pete said, as we drove onto the little beach to launch his dinghy.

He backed into the mud, and we both pulled the coconut dinghy into the water. He attached the two horse motor. He then pulled out a giant Danforth anchor. Along with it came a bunch of chain that rattled along the hitch, and thudded to the ground. I helped him pull the last of the chain out of his truck into the coconut. It had to have been 200 feet of 1/2" chain. Pete handed me a line to hold the floating coconut, while he pulled the truck around to park.

I waited, and looked around the little beach. There were thousands of little crabs running for cover under the mangroves, and a rock quarry, where a fisherman was casting a net. I saw a wooden dock, and a dilapidated house with broken windows. The dock did not connect, and was missing cross braces. I looked out to the water and could hear a sea buoy making its noise, as it tossed in the waves. I examined the river. It was a narrow strip of water with several anchored boats floating peacefully on its surface. On the other side of this narrow strip of water was a huge sand dune that followed the coast as far as I could see. The sand dune was covered with dune grass, the tide was low, and oysters spit in the grassy marsh. I continued to hear a sea buoy. It must have been on the other side of the dunes, out in the ocean. I suddenly understood that I was hearing the breaking of waves and sea.

I was suddenly fascinated with this new place I had come to. I hadn't been close to the beach since I had bought Happy. I longed for its waves ever since I had left my home on the edge of the sea.

Pete and Leelo approached. Actually, Pete was being walked by Leelo. Its legs were strong. It looked like a gremlin as it tugged on its leash. It was grunting, choking, and looking up at the trees. She began barking and coughing after a squirrel. I almost wanted to tell Pete to just let Leelo run up the tree after it!

Pete stomped by with Leelo pulling ahead, and tied her under the tree of the invading squirrel. She looked so content and alert as she stared above. I looked at Pete and back at Leelo. I was distracted by her high pitched whine and the angry chattering from the squirrel above.

I pulled my eyes away from the alien dog and saw Pete putting his oars in the dingy.

"Ready?" He untied Leelo and we all piled into the giant coconut to go out to Pete's boat.

"Is Ava going to stay with her mom during the storm?" I asked on our way out.

"Yeah. I think I will ride it out on the mooring, it seems pretty protected here, a little open from the north."

Leelo was standing with all four paws on the railing, looking at the water.

"Do you need someone out here with you, I'll help you ride out the storm," I said bravely. I didn't know why I suddenly felt so brave, when I was feeling weak hours earlier. The light was starting to fade as the sun was setting.

We arrived at Pete's boat, and I was fascinated with how different it looked. It was painted white with a green stripe, and there was no mast. There were many tarps covering the decks, and a wind generator spinning on the back. There were no lifelines, only bulwarks instead. I climbed on board with Leelo.

I walked up forward to where the anchor rode was attached. The deck was wood and what looked to be tar. The bulwarks came to a stem that stuck above to a soft point. I thought this boat looked a bit like a Viking ship, as I had noticed that the hull was lapstraked. I remembered Pete mentioning about copper being put on the bottom. It did not look to be painted, but actual copper metal hammered on.

I watched as Pete rowed his dinghy to the bow where I was standing. He pulled up the swivel that all his chain was hooked to, and shackled the new anchor chain to it. This must have been his mooring, I thought. I watched as he rowed out into the bay with the chain and anchor inside. While Pete rowed, the chain fell slowly over the side, as it was shackled to the mooring ahead.

I looked behind Pete and saw the lighthouse on the land, a black and white barber shop pole, with a light that continued to shine the way to the inlet. It circled around the harbor and lit up the sky on each rotation. The sun was setting. I could just make out the last rays shining through the stars, which were beginning to show above.

I looked back at Pete. He was rowing the coconut faster now. The chain was falling over the side of the gunnel quicker and quicker, nearing its end. I saw that the dingy was beginning to take on water from the weight of the chain. There was panic on Pete's face. He stood and ran to the other side of the coconut to stabilize it, and stop it from filling in so fast. He then quickly grabbed the anchor, and threw it over the side. Pete wiped his brow, and began bailing out the water. Soon, he rowed back to the swivel on the mooring.

"That was exciting," he said, as he tied alongside. "You ready to head back? I'm starving!"

Leelo, Pete, and I, piled into the coconut again. We were much lighter this time as the weight of chain and anchor had been tossed over. I did not understand why Leelo did not stay on board, but I did not ask anymore questions. There was only one question that was beginning to bug me.

"What is the name of your boat again, Pete?"

"Norna."

Chapter Thirteen
Tropical Storm Fay – Go Away!
-St. Augustine, Florida

Pete dropped me off at my boat behind his shop and looked a bit worried. He told me that tomorrow we needed to go to the grocery store and get some provisions for Norna, to ride out the storm the following day. I agreed, and told him I would prepare my boat also. He told me that he would help me carry my mast off my boat so it would not damage anything during the storm. I agreed that I would see him in the morning and we parted ways. Leelo barking all the way back to Pete's truck.

The next day came bright and calm; it was hard to believe that there was to be a tropical storm named Fay the next day. Pete knocked on Happy, and Leelo jumped aboard just in time to lick my face. Doodles greeted Leelo with a wagging tail, and they began their routine of chasing each other around the boat.

Pete was dressed in baggies and a paint-splattered shirt, and stood next to a man who was smoking a cigarette. Pete introduced me to him.

"Kourtney, this is Paul, he is a really good electrician, he has been doing all of the wiring on Norna."

We shook hands, "Are you here to help us move my mast off Happy?" I looked at him enthusiastically.

Paul nodded, and stubbed out his cigarette. We walked aboard, lifted my mast, and soon were carrying it behind Pete's shop.

"I thought I would do a little work this morning. If you want, you can help. After work, we should go to the grocery store and get some provisions for the storm." Pete was walking Leelo back from Happy, and tied her to the truck hitch. "Dave was supposed to come and help me today, but he had to do something."

I agreed to help Pete, and walked inside. Doodles followed behind me. Pete started undoing clamps from a gluing project and showed me how to use a hand plane. I found it fascinating to watch him work with wood.

I swept up after him and was sent next door to get sandpaper for a project. I walked into the neighboring warehouse and realized it was a place that sold to the shrimp boaters and the mariners around town. I wandered around the building with amazement at the many nets, wires and ropes it supplied, and soon found the sandpaper that Pete had sent me to get. The morning went quickly, as it was time for lunch. We piled in Pete's truck and headed to a local Mexican buffet.

I sat with Pete and started to wonder about his boat Norna. I asked him questions, as he asked me about Happy. I explained to him how I had acquired my boat, and listened to him explain to me how he had gotten Norna.

Pete's boat Norna was built by a Danish man named Flemming Boye Jorgensen. The boat was launched in 1988. It is a 37-foot (12 meter) wooden gaff-rigged cutter with a square sail. The boat has a 12 foot 6 inch (4 meter) beam, a 27-foot (9 meter) yard, and a 12 -foot (4 meter) bowsprit. Norna is lapstrake (clinker) built. She is planked with larch, and the frames are oak, with copper fastenings. Pete had redone the copper sheathed bottom. The original name of the boat was Nornegjest. It was a Danish folklore. The Folklore was something about a boy who had a candle. Norns are spirits and there are good Norns and bad Norns. One of the good Norns hid the candle from the bad Norns, because if the candle burned out, the little boy would die.

The boat, later renamed Norna, had suffered an explosion of some sort. Pete guessed maybe a propane explosion. It was a

flash fire that blew off hatches, blew up part of the coach roof, and burned the inside. The cockpit burned out, and the aft cabin was burned to a crisp. The boat was on the hard (hauled out) at a boat yard when this happened. When the fire department arrived, they found a couple pairs of shoes outside the boat. They feared someone was inside, but Flemming, the original builder, was in town.

Flemming had sailed Nornegjest from Denmark, through Trinidad and Tobago to St. Augustine, Florida. He now, after the explosion, had no home, and had to sell Nornegjest. He had apparently received insurance money for Norna, as he had sold the boat to Pete for $10. It became a good home indeed, tho it was burned and neglected for many months.

After lunch, Pete dove and fixed Happy's broken duct taped seacock valve. We decided it best to bring Doodles out to Pete's boat for the storm, and tied Happy as best we could. We bought our provisions at the grocery store, and piled into the coconut dingy. We were heading out to Norna.

I had not seen inside Pete's boat, and was surprised to find the inside gutted. There were floors, but no beds, only bunks with wood planks. There were no cushions. There was a plywood counter top with a camping stove, and a styrofoam cooler. The roof was painted white with red beams, and there was a skylight hatch in the middle that let a substantial amount of light in.

I asked Pete why there were so many canvas tarps over his boat. He explained to me that the decks were wood, and that they would move in the sun. He told me that he was planning to rake out the caulking in the seams and hammer in tarred marlin and hot tar. I sat on the wooden bunk, there was nothing but a couple sleeping bags to add cushion from the hard surface below.

We loaded his cooler with ice and food, and he began to make coffee. Leelo was, of course, chasing Doodles around the boat. Doodles skyrocketed downstairs with Leelo's face behind her. Leelo could not climb down the steep stairs, and stared at the sassy fat cat below.

There were round ports on each side of the cabin house and a big table in the middle of the companionway, with folding sides. There was a complete toilet, but no door, and no toilet paper. "Typical man", I thought to myself.

"Pete," I suggested, "I think we need to get you some cushions, and maybe a door for your bathroom."

He laughed and hung a towel over the entrance of the toilet, and replied, "Is this ok?"

"Wonderful," I said, "That's a start."

Doodles began sniffing around the boat and fell into a hole in the forward focsle. I had not noticed that there was another room in the forward part. It had no floor, which exposed the immense timbers that this vessel was made from. There were tools lying about, it looked to be a workshop of some sort. I noticed that there was no standing room in this area.

"There is also an aft cabin," Pete explained, as if reading my thoughts, "I am still in the process of fixing this up because of the explosion."

I saw his diesel engine visible under the stairs of his hatch, and I saw it was a Perkins. I could see the aft cabin through the open engine room, and saw that there were no floors or bunks. This area was gutted the most.

"I am starting to renovate the interior," Pete walked to the stove and poured a cup of coffee for me. He began explaining his ideas for the galley. I listened and offered ideas, as the night fell.

I started to hear the wind generator spin faster and the tarps began to rattle. We ran outside and took down all but one that covered the skylight. Pete wanted this one up to stop the leaks over our bunks. Little did I know that wood boats were leaky no matter what. I had to get use to this during the storm.

Leelo came down below and took over the bunks, as Norna began to tug on the anchors. Pete looked around and checked that the anchors were holding. We were in the same place, and we made ready to sleep.

Night came louder. With a howling of wind, the waves in the bay began to chop. Norna bounced and bobbed to the rhythm. We turned on the VHF and listened. The robot voice on the other end explained that the tropical storm Fay had stalled over St. Augustine. We knew we were in this for a few days. We had not provisioned enough.

"If worse comes to worse", I thought, "we will have to eat Leelo first." Doodles, meanwhile, was purring loudly and I decided it best to save her for last. The next few days became a mess of wind and waves. Each morning, we listened to the VHF, to discover that tropical storm Fay was not going away for yet another few days! We stretched our food the best we could, and luckily did not rename Leelo to "Lunch".

During this time we talked about many things, and found that we had a lot in common. Pete was a surfer, and I later discovered he surfed well. He loved bluegrass and to play his many instruments. He could play guitar, mandolin, fiddle and dobro. I sat and listened to him practice songs. When there was a lull, I called out ones for him to play while Doodles and Leelo lay together on the bunks. We bounced in the waves for several more days.

I felt a bond with Pete I hadn't felt in a long time. I decided I would help him with his boat, just as he was helping me with mine. I really felt a change in my heart for Norna. I felt at home more on this boat, than I did on Happy.

The storm passed. Pete and I could finally safely get in the coconut and ride to shore with Leelo and Doodles. As we drove to my boat Happy, I felt a sort of sadness. I wanted to stay on Norna with Pete longer. To my relief tho, through it all, Happy was safe and sound. Pete and I set to work right away to fix the cabin top.

Chapter Fourteen
I Needed a Home
-St. Augustine, Florida

I met Pete's daughter, Ava, a few days later and fell in love with her tiny voice and her happy attitude toward life, just like her dad. I saw that there was a family around me, something of which I had craved so much since the loss of my mother. I knew Pete was older than me, in fact 20 years older, but the comfort I felt with Ava and Pete astonished me. I felt at home—even more than I had when I bought Happy.

Dave came by and offered help over the next few months. We set to cutting the cabin roof off of Happy and cutting out the old balsa wood. We then put structural foam and glassed over this. With the help of the shrimp boat rigs behind Pete's shop, we reset Happy's mast. Meanwhile, Pete made his refrigerator box with 4-inches of foam. He was next ready to put the cooling plate inside. We worked filling Norna's interior with a beautiful galley and I sewed him up cushions.

Happy's cabin top was finished. Pete and I decided to live aboard Happy while we worked on Norna. We worked together to build a new mast that had been lying in the rafters of Pete's shop drying for some time. We built Norna's mast with birds mouth construction, an interesting joinery technique. Birds mouth construction is eight long pieces of wood cut into a V at forty five degree angles. When these angles are put together as a puzzle, they lock tight to form a tight, flexible bond. The outside is then shaved down with a pull saw, and rounded down smooth. The wood we used was sika spruce, and a New Zealand wood called Kauri.

I had known from the beginning that I loved Pete. He had put part-time work into Norna as he owned his wood shop, and continued to put his clients ahead of himself. He had made a good name for himself as an honest hardworking woodworker. He always tried to do his jobs in full- where I wanted to slack. Pete always pushed me to put my best efforts in. If there was anyone to be learned from, it was Pete. God knows he was always trying to teach.

Pete and I talked about crossing the Atlantic the following May. We had found this to be a dream we both shared. It felt like the right time. The economy was crashing in America, and people were losing work. We knew we could not bring Ava, it was too heavy a trip. We knew it was to be our first-time crossing and we felt lucky that Ava could stay at home with her mother, but knew we would miss her terribly.

Months later, I decided to sell Happy to Pete's friend Paul -the man who had helped carry my mast off onto land. I could not thank him enough, as I was beginning to wonder if I could sell Happy before we would be making the crossing in a few months to come.

I knew that Happy was a home I could look forward to go to. I had named my boat Happy, because it was the one Happiness I could find in knowing stability. I felt that I, at least, had Happy to come home to, that I had a home. Since I had met Pete and Ava, I knew I had found one. I needed a home.

Before I had met Pete, before I had even found my sailboat Happy, I had lost my mother at a young age. This had led to several other problems.

I had quit having my period and started producing breast milk when I was about 16. I was living in a foster home at the time with a woman named Tammy and her husband Keith. They were great people who taught me Christianity and the love of Jesus. Tammy brought me to a doctor, and I found out that I had some weird hormonal problem. I was given a CAT scan. The doctors found that I had a mass in my brain, on my pituitary gland, that was making my body think it was pregnant.

Previously, I had been made to take an anti-psychotic medicine, because I was having a hard time with the death of my mother. She died from cancer when I was 14. She suffered for years with this disease. Her life ended with her in the hospital, and us holding her hand as we said goodbye. My mother was only 54 years old.

The years that followed had become a blur. My dad was exceptionally hurt by the loss of his wife. He loved her, though, he had been seduced by a new woman. The new woman came to help around the house after the death, but I soon found them to be dating. They began dating two months after the trauma I experienced. My sister couldn't take it, and left the house.

This new woman and I did not get along. My dad and she wed a year later. She started talking negatively, saying that we were spoiled. We *were* spoiled, but at 15, puberty, and trying not to cry at the thought of the loss of my mother, I could not hear this too. The woman and I had fought so much that, eventually, my dad was persuaded to put me into a group home.

I lived in the group home for a year, went to an alternative school, and soon moved into the foster home, where I learned of my hormonal false pregnancy. The medicine I took at 14 was what could have caused my infertility.

This woman and my dad divorced after only two years. This was long enough for her to convince the courts that she owned part of the house I had lived in my whole life, and part of my dad's hard-earned money.

My dad and I did not talk for a long time after all that had happened. It was not until I decided to sail the Atlantic, that my dad could open up, and say what was in his heart. My dad needed to say these things, because I wanted him to know, I forgave him a long time ago.

"Kourtney, you know, your mothers death took a lot out of me."

I began to cry, trying to hold in the tears as my dad talked to me. I remember him crying on my shoulder as mom was lying in the hospital, going to see her every day after school. My dad was so lost.

"It took a lot out of all of us, dad."

"I know, well, I put you in that group home, and," there was a long pause, I knew he had felt some guilt, "and you were so hurt, the counselor told me it would make you stronger."

I couldn't believe my dad was finally getting these things off his chest.

"Dad, that was the best thing you could have done for me, I was hurting, and I needed something to let me see I was not alone."

I could hear my dad begin to cry. I had seen so many girls that had been in situations worse than mine in that home.

"I, I have been, I am proud of you Kourtney, you went from, hell, getting lost in downtown St. Petersburg, to traveling across the world."

I cried, but laughed at the memory of when I got lost, "I was so lost after my graduation, St.

Petersburg is so easy to find your way around, just go around the block, and I was so lost." I blew my nose. "Thank you dad."

"You know Kourtney, you don't have to do this, but just know you always have a home here."

Hearing this from my dad made my days easier and brighter. At that moment I felt a huge weight lifted off my chest. My dad had finally said what he needed to, and I finally found peace in knowing that my dad was proud of me.

Chapter Fifteen
The Preparedness
-St. Augustine, Florida

The next few months were a blur of preparing for an Atlantic crossing. We had stocked Norna to the brim with as much food as we thought we would need. I did not know what would taste good offshore. I tried my best to follow advice of people who had experience in blue water sailing.

I had learned that bananas were meant to hang away from any other fruits and vegetables, because they would gas off, and make everything gas off too. This meant that all of our fruit and veggies would ripen and rot. I had also learned that eggs could be unrefrigerated as long as they were fresh and flipped every day. We also boiled several eggs. I had learned to peel the old skin off onions, so that they could grow new ones and not mold up. I bought raw meat, which later, I had regretted.

We had decided it best to give Leelo and Doodles to a good home, because of the formalities of bringing pets overseas. Doodles went to a canvas shop. Leelo went with a man in North Carolina, where she could run under the trees, and chase squirrels all she wanted, without worrying about cars.

The last few days before leaving, became a fury of emotions and recollection. We hugged Ava tight, and told her we would call her in a month. She was brave and did not cry. She had given us a positive happiness that we could look forward to her flying over and seeing us in Europe.

We did not know if we were going to die out there. Or what we would encounter. We had spent the last few days trying to breathe easy, and calm our nerves. I was especially nervous of being seasick, as I did not know if I was ready to be tossed around dizzy. I tried my best to sleep the night before our departure, as my worries and memories quickly flooded back.

I thought back to the first time I really went sailing (besides sailing Bipolar with an umbrella). This time was on an 18-foot sprit-rigged boat named "Little Bird" that Pete had built for Ava.

The day I went sailing, I sailed alone. The plan was that I was to sail "Little Bird" to the mothership, Norna, at anchor. Pete, then would launch his dinghy, and meet me on Norna, with Little Bird tied alongside. Pete thought I had more experience sailing, though it wasn't his fault. I was novice enough, to even consider sailing my dinghy Bipolar with an umbrella, as experience enough.

Pete pushed me off to sail Little Bird alone. I was really going along with a brisk wind, and I held tight onto the tiller. I had to brace myself on the boat, as I was afraid it would flip. (Later, I learned from Pete, that Little Bird couldn't flip. He had made it that way for his daughter, Ava, to sail by herself).

I sailed along in the brisk wind, and quickly made it to Norna- the mother ship. Unfortunately, I did not know what to do when I got there. I didn't know how to stop! I hit Norna, and fell out of the little sailing boat. After surfacing, I watched it sail away without me.

A couple minutes later, Pete rowed out. He looked from me in the water, to his beautiful "Little Bird" sailing away. He admitted to me later that he was unsure who to go for first. Lucky for me, Pete rowed over, pulled me in his dingy, and we rescued Little Bird together.

This was my first experience sailing. Two great lessons were learned. Pete, immediately after rescuing Little Bird, taught me to stop the boat. This required loosening the sail and letting it fly, or even pointing into the wind, and letting the sail flap. He also made sure I understood never to fall off the boat, and to stay onboard at all times. These lessons were learned by me in earnest (and the hard way).

I knew, with these small experiences, I was to awaken the next morning, untie our dock lines, and sail Norna out the St. Augustine, Florida inlet. Pete and I, aboard Norna, planned to cross the Atlantic Ocean. To cross to a country on the other side.

Chapter Sixteen
Universal Language
> **-Spain**

The morning came bright and calm. I awoke with a start. Pete was awake before me making breakfast. He was as jittery as me. We knew we were going to fire up the engine, to motor offshore in an hour.

"Our plan was to sail across the North Atlantic, above Bermuda and the Azores and land in Ireland. We had left on May 30th, as we learned that this was the best time of year to make such a crossing."
– Diary Entry May 30th 2010

We untied the dock lines after breakfast.

After an hour motoring out the inlet and setting the sails, we sat to rest and adjust to the movement of the ocean. I do not remember most of the first day. I think I was mostly in shock. It was mostly a blur.

A few days went by as we went north, following up the coast of America. The anxiety level began to fall, though I was feeling very seasick. We went past Georgia, South Carolina, then North Carolina. We then became uncomfortably close to Cape Fear and the Frying Pan Shoals. This was when we knew it was time to head east, on a compass course to Europe.

I had not eaten, or slept very well. I felt very weak because of being seasick. I had a panic attack and told Pete I was too afraid to head east, that I wanted to go back to land. It was then that I realized it would take a few days to even get to land. We were already two days offshore. At that moment, I was not going to instantly be where I wanted to be.

It was a scary feeling. It was a moment of realization that I was really far away from anything. It was no longer a change of scenery that was going to make me feel better. I needed to mentally handle my fear, and to force myself to sleep. I needed sleep.

I slept, and awoke feeling better and refreshed. I then forced food down, and felt strength come back. Dolphins came to play off the bow. Pete asked me again if I was ready to head east. I no longer felt the anxiety I had the night before. I nodded, "Let's go."

We turned into the Gulf Stream. Pete and I both knew we had entered into it, because the waves were even bigger than on the coast. There was nothing but horizon from all sides. Nothing blocked the view of what was ahead, except the curve of the earth.

As the sun set, the wind gradually died down. The waves subsided. We found ourselves with full sails slapping in the calm ocean swell. We then sailed into a red mist. It was an abyss of setting sun and fog. I looked out the starboard side, and noticed a fishing boat amongst the calmness. We were Inside a giant bubble of fog. Nothing but the fishing boat and us, two ghost ships, drifting in a magnetic current. This current was pulling us farther and farther out to sea.

That night, after turning into the Gulf Stream to head east across the Atlantic, I dreamed of Happy, and of the first time I had anchored out in a harbor.

My friends had helped move Happy to the south-side anchorage in downtown St. Augustine. They had put me on an old mooring. I went into work the next day, and when I returned saw my boat was not where I had left it!

A man named Less contacted me. He brought me to the city marina, where my boat had drifted right into a dock slip. Happy had drifted right next to a gaff-rigged skipjack called "Music", and Less was the Captain. A few days after the incident, and after I safely anchored Happy back in the anchorage, Less contacted me again. He asked if I would like to help sail Music, to take some pictures of it for the advertisement of his business.

It was as though Happy had drifted in the dock slip next to Music, to show me I belonged on gaff-rigged ships. Little did I know I would find myself sailing across the Atlantic on a wooden gaff rigged cutter with a square sail, named Norna.

During my dream of Happy and my much needed sleep, Pete kept awake dutifully for his watch. Because it was only two of us, we shared the tasks of cooking and maintenance, as well as taking three-hour watches. During a "watch", one person stayed awake and kept an eye on the horizon and sails, while the other rested. Whoever was on watch checked the horizon every 15 minutes to ensure no ships had appeared. We also continued to check that Norna was moving fast enough. It was always important to continue moving.

As we headed east farther and farther away from Florida, I saw a bright star that I later learned was the shoulder of Taurus. I noticed that the bright star was connected to a triangle. It looked as though the triangle was pointing to Florida. When it was time, Taurus showed us the way back home. (I later followed this star, watching it in the night sky, during my watches. I followed it all the way back, through the Caribbean.)

Pete and I slowly made our way east at an average speed of 5 knots. As each offshore day passed, I became use to waking up and looking out at blue horizons, shimmering in the bright reflection of water. One morning, however, I had a moment where I couldn't differentiate between the two. I woke up from a deep sleep and popped my head outside. Pete was sitting up on deck with his eyes closed. The sun was high in the sky. I looked at the blue around me, and I did not know where the sky and the water met. I could not find a horizon! This loss of knowing which way was up, put me in a quick panic. I soon found my bearings and focused on the earths curve. What an amazing blue world we live in.

The night stars had more depth than I ever knew possible. I never knew that light pollution had such a great effect on seeing the real sky, until sailing in the middle of the Atlantic. The stars completely filled each space, in the dark matter between. There were layers that I had never seen - milky ways that glowed brilliantly. The seven sisters constellation danced bright amongst the vast glow. This amazing canvas of stars touched the horizon.

I loved night watches. I often let Pete sleep longer, just so that I could lay on deck and absorb the star light. This vastness of the ocean will never leave my mind. I will always remember how much space there is, in such a blue living thing. I later canvassed a painting of Norna sailing. She had a full mainsail, and both inner and outer jibs flying strong. I placed Norna as tiny as I could, and set her with a backdrop of blue sky and ocean - of clouds and reflection.

We landed in Bermuda after 10 days. We landed at night, which was not recommended in any of our charts. We worked our way through the lit buoys of St. George harbor in Bermuda, to anchor in the channel with an overheating motor.

We had decided to stop in Bermuda, because we had heavy weather blasting to the north of us. We sailed south to avoid this. As we reefed and tacked to head south to Bermuda, we had torn our mainsail. We did not know how the mainsail tore, but we assumed that we did not reef it correctly. It tore at the stitching. The sails were tired and old. They should have been replaced before we left.

We spent the next couple days in Bermuda, waiting for our torn mainsail to be repaired, and called home. Ava's little voice came over the internet. We were already beginning to miss her. Pete and I knew we had to leave quickly to avoid hurricanes. After more provisioning and rerigging of our mainsail, we set out for the next leg of our journey.

About 15 days from Bermuda, we experienced thick fog. During this time, we relied on our radar, to tell us if there were ships nearby. We stood our watches. Only problem this time, was that we did not know there was fog.

We had decided, after getting comfortable with being offshore, that we would sleep together during the daytime. We would, however, be strict with our night watches. It was decided that I was better at staying awake during the night, but we had to stick with four hour shifts in order to keep evenly rested. Pete was on his turn for night watch, and I went below. By daybreak, we both were sleeping.

A fog horn blasted.

Pete and I groggily laid for a minute longer, and heard the fog horn blast again. At first, I wondered why we were hearing a fog horn blast. I began to doze off, when Pete sat up like a spring. It finally had dawned on me, we were out in the middle of the Atlantic! A ship!

Pete scrambled out of bed and looked out the hatch. A thick gray mist intruded the air. We could not see to the end of Norna. We both stumbled down the companionway stairs to the radar. We saw nothing of a ship. We turned the radar higher and saw nothing still.

Pete fumbled for the VHF, and called the ship, giving our coordinates. While talking on the VHF, Pete absentmindedly blew his fog horn.

We sat, nervously waiting on edge of what was bearing down on us, on the other side of the foggy barrier. We saw and heard nothing again. Nothing showed on radar, and there was no reply on VHF. The ship was gone.

Pete laid back down with me after much nervousness and anticipation. After several minutes, I began to laugh.

"What? What's so funny?" Pete asked me.

I laughed out again, "Did you blast the fog horn *while* you were talking on VHF? If you did, do you realize that you *may* have been blasting the horn into the VHF radio at them?"

Pete blinked and realized he might have. "Someone got a loud wake up call."

"Unfortunately - for our travel across the Atlantic, the year was exceptionally stormy to the north and would not allow us to head above Latitude 45 - which is where we need to be in order to get to Ireland. During this time we sailed 10 days to Bermuda. After 34 days at sea, we arrived in Baiona, Spain. 4,000 miles logged, and only 40 gallons of fuel used.
- Diary Entry July 4, 2010

BAIONA, SPAIN

We Saw Baiona on July 15. We first saw the Isle of Cies at the entrance. To my surprise, the fog was lifting and the waves were calming. We were entering a harbor!

This was when panic set in. We were entering a harbor! We hadn't seen land for 34 days. We were pulling into an unknown harbor, in an unknown country, for the first time. Maybe it was not panic necessarily. Maybe it was more of anxiety, or nervousness, or even, a feeling without explanation. I was relieved to see land. No matter what the feeling was, I was smiling from ear to ear.

We stepped onto land and noticed that everyone was having a normal day. The locals were not looking at us, they were doing their own thing, walking about, and talking in Spanish.

We were approached by the dock master. He explained to us that it was siesta, and that we had to wait to fill out the forms with the customs authority. He pointed to a restaurant across the street that sold Kebobs. We must have looked hungry.

We ate with gusto. Pete's beard was so full of food, that he looked like he had rolled in his plate. I had eaten so fast, I didn't feel full.

We had finally found land. Though it was not Ireland, our original plan, we were happy to be safe. Pete and I had successfully completed a blue water sail.

"Ava, her grandfather Jim, and her grandmother Margaret, came to visit us for two weeks. Ava was so excited to see her dad. It had been two months. Pete was anxious to give her a hug. We showed them around town, through the beautiful backstreets. We showed her the granite rocks and the huge mountains."
- Diary Entry August 14, 2010

COMBARRO, SPAIN

We took Ava and the family sailing to a "cala" north of Baiona, called Combarro. Combarro was having a wooden boat "Fiesta Do Mar" (Festival by the Sea). The dock master of this Fiesta, offered free dockage for two days and three days free food, if we would stay, and have Norna sail in the festival also. They offered huge plates of piaia, squid, octopus, and fried sardines. We were very hungry sailors after not having fresh food offshore.

Pete and I had an amazing time with Ava and the family during the Fiesta. We watched sailors dock while playing the bagpipes. We saw hundreds of wooden boats sail in the beautiful bay, amongst the backdrop of mountainsides and vineyards. We tried all of the local flavor, and watched fireworks right over the boat.

Norna even sailed around the harbor with the wooden boats. There were traditional rigged boats everywhere, lateen rigs, gaff rigs, and dipping lug rigs. Norna fit right in.

I stayed on the dock and took pictures of Norna, as we had no pictures of her sailing. We enjoyed our time showing off all the hard work we put into her to all the wooden boat lovers. Pete and I also played a little music with the locals. Music was the universal language.

"Ava and the family had a great time exploring Northern Spain. We sadly watched them go home, and knew we would see Ava soon. Suddenly, a bit of fear came to me. We were far away from home. I could not let this fear overtake me. I knew that in order to enjoy this trip, I would have to put fear

out of my mind. Pete and I had to try to do our best to make our way around safely."

- Diary Entry August 31, 2010

Chapter Seventeen
A Fearful Anchoring & Broken Rig
-Portugal & Spain

"Our plan- once we landed in Baiona, Spain- was to cruise down the coast of Portugal. We had to do so quickly, as winter was two months away, and fast approaching. Pete and I decided to sail into the Mediterranean. We wanted to get as far east before winter approached. We had a year to tour around Europe."
–Diary Entry August 31, 2010

NAZARE, PORTUGAL
August 31, we headed down the coast. We landed in Nazare September 4.

During our trip to Nazare, down the coast of Portugal, I saw the green flash. The green flash is a natural phenomenon that few people get to see. It is a light spectrum that happens very quickly as the sun touches the horizon and mixes with the atmosphere. As the sun dips below the horizon, a green flash appears where the sun's rays once shone.

On this journey, I also had found that my seasickness was not nearly as harsh. I wasn't sick for five days, like I was when I first left St. Augustine Florida. Instead, I was sick for the first two days. It would tire me out, and I had to sleep a little longer. I could not go down below to cook. This commenced until my body became balanced, and I 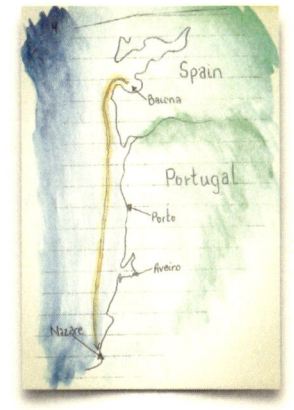 could see straight enough to walk around deck. Once the two days passed, I felt less queasy and could go down below and cook Pete a meal. Pete was very patient with me during this time, and I continued to keep good watches, to show my appreciation.

Nazare is a small fishing village with extremely excellent food. After 43 days crossing the Atlantic, Pete and I decided that living is all about food, not only eating it, but the variety of it.

During our Atlantic crossing, I did not stock us up as well as I had anticipated. I had considered beans and rice sufficient enough, as I thought we would catch more fish. Little did we know, we would not get as much variety as we thought. During the last week of our Atlantic crossing, we had beans and rice for breakfast, lunch, and dinner. I lost so much weight, that I could fit into Ava's clothes.

Pete and I really enjoyed Nazare. It was a magical, gorgeous place with wonderful ocean-washed beaches and dunes. This backdrop was set in the bountiful sea. Nazare's cuisine was mainly from the sea. We inhaled fish stews, olives and pates.

Some of the ports, such as Nazare, were small coves that were cut into the beach and lined with piles of man-made rock barriers. We knew we did not want to stay long on the coast of Portugal, as ports were few and far between. The beaches were vast, surrounded by dunes and cliffs. The coast showed that the weather could give a good beating if it wanted to.

BERLINGA ISLANDS, PORTUGAL

We sailed to the Berlinga Islands, just off of Peniche, Portugal, where we anchored for the night. It was a beautiful island with caves and polka-dotted lizards. The cliffs were red and the water was crystal clear with brilliant blues. This clear water reflected light on the caves surrounding the bottom of the cliffs. There was a monastery set on a rock hill.

Anchoring off these islands was very harsh during the night. The wind picked up and the waves wrapped around the red rocks. Norna tossed and bounced and tugged on the anchor. Pete and I stayed on watch because of the fear of dragging. The jagged rocks sat like teeth, while the white waves crashed on them in the moonlight.

We were compromised, because we did not have the dinghy on the davits. Earlier that day we rowed into shore to climb the top and look out over the vast view beyond. The problem was that the line to the dinghy was behind Norna. Pete feared that if we had to motor away from the jagged teeth in the night, we might get the dinghy line wrapped around the prop. To compound our situation further, we could not pull the thrashing dinghy onto the davits. Trying to climb into the rocking and violent boat would be too dangerous, and near impossible.

We watched a boat anchored near us struggle to pull up its anchor, in the thrashing and bouncing seas. I sat in fear, while watching the waves crash into the rocks. The moonlight cast enough light to see the white rolling foam of the rough raging waters. The man in the boat next to us worked vigorously. He fell against his cabin side several times, as he slipped and rolled from the angry seas. He worked for a good hour, slowly clinking his chain up with each lurch. Finally his anchor pulled from the stubborn hold, and he slowly motored away from sight.

Pete and I were afraid to pull our anchor. We did not have an electric windlass. The windlass we had was excruciatingly slow. It would pull up only one chain link at a time. The ground tackle holding Norna was around 30 feet of 3/8" chain, about 150 chain links. The 65 pound CQR added a substantial amount of weight. We knew we were in danger.

Pete and I sat awake the whole night. We kept our watches until the wind and waves subsided. It was then that we could rest comfortably in the last few hours before sunlight. I had never felt so relieved to see the sun before this day.

CHIPIONA, SPAIN

It was now September 16. We had an amazing and relaxing sail to Cape St. Vincent, while being pulled along by our square sails. After the scary night by the jagged teeth of the Berlinga Islands, Pete and I took turns to catch up on much needed sleep.

Pete and I had decided we would anchor at Cape St. Vincent, the very pointy chin of Portugal, and also the farthest point West in Europe.

We arrived at the chin of Portugal, to the flat, wind-carved rocks of Cape St. Vincent, the following day. To our disappointment, we saw a thunderstorm over the cape. We knew that we would have to ride out another storm next to jagged teeth again, and set a course to continue on. We decided to go to the underside of Portugal, into what is called the Algarve.

As Pete and I sailed past Cape St. Vincent, the wind was slightly off our starboard stern. We contemplated between flying our square sails, or keeping the outer jib we had already set. The square sails were perfect for steady following winds and seas. The outer jib was our power sail, it flew off our 12 foot bowsprit, and was manageable during any shifts of wind. Most capes could be a notorious place for these shifts.

Pete decided to leave up the outer jib, and we both were very glad we did, because once we rounded the chin, the wind picked up to 25-30 knots.

In order to get Norna sailing steady with our main and jibs up, we needed 20 knots of wind. In fact, Norna rode really well at 25-30 knots of wind, with just a jib. Square sails would have been frightening trying to put up, as they were for lighter wind. They could ride through 25-30 knots, but not without a fight when putting them up.

The wind picked up, and we felt confident that sailing with just a jib was fine and dandy.

Pete went below to cook dinner and I followed him below to pee. As soon as we both went off watch, we heard a loud BANG! We both ran on deck to see what had happened. We looked in the water first. Had Norna hit something? a whale? a submarine? a log floating in the water? We saw nothing. We checked the bilges, everything was fine. We next assumed something in the bowsprit might have broken. We, at one point, did break a turnbuckle in the North Atlantic. Nothing. Bowsprit looked fine. We looked all over the boat. It must have been a weird wave.

I assumed it was a freak noise and took my usual watch. Pete, on the other hand, was not convinced. After dinner, Pete went on deck and began checking the rigging and the sails. He then noticed the rigging on the port side was very loose. He found what the loud BANG was! Two 3/8 inch (10mm) stainless steel standing rigging cables (the cables that hold the mast up), had given way! Not one, but two! We had one more standing rigging cable holding our mast from falling to its doom on the port side. It was not blowing THAT hard!

Norna's standing rigging was a dead eye system, along with a gaff-rigged mainsail. This sail configuration was not stressful on the standing rigging. We did notice, however, that the rigging flexed while under sail, probably because of the dead-eye system. Norna's rigging cables broke from metal fatigue, because of the constant tugging and pulling of offshore cruising. I was learning a lot.

Pete jerry-rigged the mainsail block and tackle to the broken side, and used this as a crutch to hold the mast from falling down.

Our next decision was to find a place to stop in the Algarve. We searched our cruising guide and read that many places were not easy to enter. There were ripping currents in many of the rivers of the Algarve. Our motor, still named "The Terrorist", was still leaking antifreeze. We did not want to push the engine too hard, while trying to work against these currents. The easiest place to enter was Chipiona, another day into our trip. I had a good feeling about Chipiona, it sounded like a happy name. We needed some cheering up. We turned The Terrorist on, and miserably made our way east.

Our spirits were down. What were we going to do? Pete took a look at the stainless rigging and knew it was getting old. It had been parceled and serviced very well, which meant a "lifetime cable". We later learned the reason for the metal fatigue. Stainless required oxygen. To properly parcel and serve standing rigging, the cable would be galvanized, as oxygen is not required. Stainless without oxygen will become brittle, and as we found, will break.

September 19, we were blessed to dock next to a man named Fernando, in Chipiona, Spain. He spoke English very well, and understood we were on a tight cruising budget.
Fernando took us to a warehouse with wholesale prices. We bought galvanized cable, and everything needed to fix our rigging. We also bought extra to replace the other side. Thanks to Fernando, Norna could sail again.

Chapter Eighteen
Mistrals Angry Little Sister
-Sardinia, Italy

After the many repairs from the breaking of our rig, we sailed into the Mediterranean with fresh strong breezes right behind us. Winter was fast approaching.
I couldn't believe it! We were in the Mediterranean Sea! I saw an owl, a submarine, pilot whales, and strange fuzzy things floating across the water. Norna was about to cross 0' Longitude.

"I have been learning so much. I understand how the universal time clock works for navigating. Our boat will be on the other side of the Greenwich Mean Time, or 0' Longitude! To put it into perspective, when we left Florida, we were at about 80' Longitude. Each degree of time has minutes, which is 60 minutes on each degree. There is 1000 seconds on each minute. This makes it 6000 times farther than just 80'. We spent all this time counting down to zero, to count back up!
–Diary Entry September 23, 2010

SARDINIA, ITALY

"Pete and I sailed past Gibraltar, Morocco, and the Balearic Islands. We sailed five days to Sardinia, Italy. We wanted to get as far into the Mediterranean as we could, before winter set in. We knew on our way back west, back out of the neck of Gibraltar, that we could explore any places we passed. Sardinia was the windiest place I've ever experienced. It was in the time space continuum of the Gulfe Du Lion.

The Gulfe Du Lion is the accumulation of storms that blast across the Atlantic into the Bay of Biscay. These named winds travel through the Alps and funnel either to the Balearic Sea, or through the Strait of Bonifacio, between northern Sardinia and Corsica. This was right where we were. Pete and I experienced several scary nights of furious winds from perfectly clear skies. We saw many tiny water tornados speeding across the bay, as the howling rush of air moved noisily through the trees.

**During this ferocious blast of air, Pete
and I stood butt naked on the bow of
Norna, watching the amazing act of
Nature. We stood helplessly, holding
tight, as Norna bucked sideways by
gusts off the inverted mountains. The
wind we experienced from the
direction of the Gulfe Du Lion, was
called a Mistral."
–Diary Entry, September 30, 2010**

About 30 miles before landing in northwest
Sardinia, the wind switched on our nose. Pete
and I spent the next morning and night pounding
into waves, and trying to push through the
Mistral. It did not want us to go to land.

It was painful to see land, smell the pine
trees, and to not be able to reach our destination.
We had already sailed five days. Trying to point
Norna into the wind was a fantastic and wet ride,
and we were getting weary. Norna did not like the
fight, and she creaked and groaned under strain.
We would not ordinarily fight the wind, but we
were being pushed back out to sea, so terribly
close to our destination.

Pete tried tacking back and forth, instead of
pointing directly into the offensive wind. We were
getting nowhere whichever way we tried. We
sailed around in the wrong direction for a day

and a half. The wind finally allowed us to head toward the dark mountains in the distance, and we safely made our way toward land.

We arrived in Porto Conte, Sardinia. It was a beautiful landlocked bay, with green hinder land, and rainbows. We breathed in the mountain air, and longingly looked at the green hills by the water. We were so happy to be by land! We later explored the unspoiled beauty of the wind carved paradise, and stayed in this area for nine months. This is not to mention that the weather kept us there, as winter was on its way.

PORTO CONTE, SARDINIA

After arriving to the safety of land, Pete and I decided we would anchor for the night in the first cove. It was open to the south, but we knew we could move to the next bay farther in and find protection, if we needed.

We anchored for the night and fell asleep, to only awaken an hour later. It was thundering and lightning, and the seas were crashing against rocks. We were already exhausted from our battle with opposing winds and seas, and knew we had to stay awake longer to motor Norna into the safety of the next bay.

We pulled up anchor, and motored into the waves. I could see wave crests breaking foamy white water, as we motored dangerously close to a lee shore. Norna sloshed around side-to the breaking waves, and slide down the faces.

My feet slipped on the deck, as I hung tight to the tiller. Several times, I slid down the aft cabin deck, as the boat lurched and rolled. As I slid, I continued to hold tight to the tiller, and the boat pitched and jumped from my sudden lack of control on the helm. I positioned myself back, only to be thrown again into the dodger pole. My harness was the only thing between me, and falling into the waves.

As I screamed forward to Pete, I could only hear my voice carried away. Pete could not hear my screams; he was busy fighting with the dangling anchor, still not in its place in the bow roller. He tugged and heaved steadily, as we slid again down another breaking wave. The crest water broke into the cockpit.

I throttled The Terrorist forward with more speed to motor away from the teeth, and slid down the deck again, as a wave crest rolled over me. I looked toward the land I was trying to get away from, the very same land we fought to get to. I watched the waves break on the rocks, the same rocks that were dangerously close to our vessel. How ironic, I thought.

I held on tight to the tiller and watched as Pete crawled aft, toward me to take over the helm. He must have finished. He instructed me to run below deck and ensure the bilge pumps were pumping water out. Norna, being a wood boat, always kept the same thought in the back of our minds. We needed to check our bilges to ensure that she was not taking any water. She did not leak terribly, in fact none at all, but it was always a concern, no matter. We definitely didn't need this, on top of everything else.

I checked the bilges and the chart as we thrashed, holding onto to every handle I could find. After plotting our position on the chart, I found that we were far enough away from the dangerous jagged teeth. We could straighten our position, and run with the waves to enter into the safety of the harbor.

I climbed up the hatchway to ensure Pete of this. As we turned with the waves, the lurching stopped and Norna swayed side to side, the waves following. Finally, after over 24 hours of being awake, being forced to thrash in mistral winds and waves; we could safely and slowly find ourselves in a calm bay.

We anchored, gently rocked, and listened to the waves in the next bay over. We were wide awake from the excitement. After being awake for so long, and feeling a sort of supernatural sleep deprivation, we quieted down our nervousness, to hear donkeys calling and birds chirping.

~~~~~~~~~

During our stay in Sardinia, we found that the town of Alghero, a few miles away, offered a free dock during Mistrals. Every time we heard of a strong Mistral blowing, we would sail from Porto Conte, and dock at the Town Quay in Alghero.

Pete and I also needed to fix our diesel, as it was still leaking anti-freeze, and overheating. We learned we had a blown head gasket. This was what was making the antifreeze overflow out of "The Terrorist"!

We met a man named Franco and his wife Gilda, during our stay in Alghero. Soon we were friends with him and his wife, and had several nights of pizza aboard Norna.

Franco was a Perkins dealer and he helped us get a new head gasket for our engine.

Once we received the gasket, Pete and I spent several days and long nights pulling apart our engine and replacing the problem. After Franco adjusted our valves, The Terrorist was no longer an overheating problem and was renamed "Perky".

> **"November - After a couple months of getting to know our surroundings, we hauled Norna at a place called Fertilia. Pete nailed replacement copper pieces, with tar and tar paper, to any corroded places on her bottom. As I helped, I learned what Pete meant when he told me about the coppering on Norna. We both lived off of spaghetti and homemade soup, in the boat yard of Fertillia, as winter quickly arrived. We collected driftwood off the beach every day to put in our wood burning stove. This kept us warm on the rainy, stormy nights, as we heated hot water bottles to put in our beds, and hot tea to warm our belly. My dad and stepmom flew us home for the month of December and the New Year."**
> **-Diary Entry, December 31,2010 – January 1, 2011**

Chapter Nineteen
The Angry Landlubber
-Sardinia, Italy and Corsica, France

"We spent our visit home with Ava and family, and a month later stepped on the plane back to our wooden home in Sardinia. February of 2011, we put her back in the water. I bought new tanbark sails from Hong Kong and prepared to have Ava fly in to see us in Sardinia for her summer break.

During this time, there was a lot of political unrest in northern Africa. There was a war in Libya, the people were protesting to cast out their dictator. Because of this, Ava could not fly over to see us, so we rescheduled her flight to see us in the Caribbean. This would be during her spring break the following year. Pete was upset he would not get to hug Ava for

several months. We missed her
already.

Pete and I cruised around the
north of Sardinia, and saw a little
of Corsica before heading back
west. We needed to scoot out to
the Balearics at a time when the
weather was not blowing at us
from the Gulfe Du Lion.

We wanted to be to the Canaries
off of the coast of Africa before
September of 2011. We had six
months to cruise the
Mediterranean."
–Diary Entry, May 28, 2011

Castelsardo, Sardinia

After repairing Perky's head gasket, we
sailed around the top of Sardinia, through the
Fornelli Passage, and anchored in crystal clear
blue water. We woke up at four in the morning
the next morning. There were perfect winds to
blow us to Castelsardo, it was about a seven
hour trip away.

We sailed Norna all the way, rolling and
pitching, a most uncomfortable, seasick ride. To
my amazement though, I had no seasickness,

and I could even go down below to cook. We had tuna fish, something of which would make me green. I was happy to know that over time, my nerves were becoming stronger.

We were tired and weary after a long, seven hour day of sailing. We constantly needed to brace ourselves from the rolly swells. We also needed to prepare ourselves for an exciting ride into a safe port.

Castelsardo harbor was a frightening place to motor into, because of the wind direction that changed upon our arrival. Waves built from this wind fetch, and the only way to enter the harbor was to surf into it! We surfed our 10 ton heavy displacement sailboat on 3 foot (1 meter) waves, into the tiny harbor of Castelsardo.

Upon arrival, Pete and I anxiously pulled up to the fuel dock, and tied Norna alongside. I stood on the dock waiting for a fuel tender to arrive, and watched several fishing boats surf into the difficult harbor entrance. I was very happy to be still, and starving from our long rolly day of sailing.

Several minutes later, I heard a woman yelling at Pete outside as I was making lunch. I stepped on deck, and saw a thin woman standing on the fuel dock, yelling for us to move.

She screamed very loudly in broken English that we had to pay for a dock with electric and water (we needed neither, we just needed fuel). The wind was blowing 30 knots straight onto the dock we were on. Pete and I looked at each other, there was no way we could move off this dock without bow thrusters. After surfing into the harbor, we could not leave, enough was enough.

I looked at the woman, as she continued to yell, and became increasingly annoyed by her ignorance for the difficulties of being a sailor. We couldn't leave right when she demanded, we needed fuel, both for the boat, and ourselves.

I spoke to her in broken Italian that we were very tired and hungry. I tried explaining, with hand gestures, that we had heard the town offered a free night's stay.

She continued yelling at us in Italian. I interpreted that she demanded us to call the port captain, and ask him if we could stay. I spoke back to her in broken Italian that we had no phone, that we were American, and visiting her country.

The woman looked at me, after yelling at us in Italian the entire time, and proceeded to say in perfect English "Oh, so you have no phones in America?"

I looked at her and her sarcasm; this woman could speak English the whole time.

I looked over at Pete. He was taking the beating after being awake for a very long day, and was not going to argue back. We had to eat first.

I grabbed Pete's hand and sat him down to eat lunch, as the lady continued to yell outside. She began knocking on our hull.

I stopped my lunch.

I was done being yelled at.

I walked outside and yelled "No, we are staying here," in the best Italian I could muster.

She looked at me with surprise. This woman finally got the point. She stepped in her car, and drove away.

We had a terrible impression of Castelsardo after this. We walked to the port captain straight away, after gulping down our cold lunch, and explained the situation. The captain of the harbor was very relaxed and professional and told us everything was OK and to stay, that a free day was offered.

Pete and I shook off the bad energy, and enjoyed our stay in Castelsardo without further incident. We left the next morning and anchored in a nearby bay called Liscia.

Liscia bay was beautiful. It was a sand dune beach that rolled right down to the anchorage. The water was crystal clear, we could see our anchor on the bottom. There was a river we drifted into on the coconut dinghy. We saw wading birds and land turtles that plowed through the undergrowth in search of food. After resting, we planned to sail to a park, north of Liscia, the next morning.

The park was named La Maddalena. The service was strict about black and grey holding tanks, and rightly so, to protect the wildlife within its boundaries. We decided while we were in Liscia Bay, we would ensure our holding tank and macerator pump was working. We had found that a lot of ports in Italy did not offer any sort of pump out facility, so we used a bucket for pee, and bagged our "other." Oh the pity of sail boaters, and boaters alike, who deal with such wastes, and smell it too.

Pete ran saltwater through the toilet, and decided to prime the macerator in a bucket. Of course, the macerator pump would not prime. Next, Pete unhooked the hose from the holding tank, stuck it into the bucket, and tried again to force a prime. The macerator began to work! Pete looked over at me, and I stood to flip the switch for the pump. Suddenly, we heard a crack! Black water was splashing from the macerator. It had just exploded! We had disgusting macerator water leaking on everything in the space it was in.

Thus began a very long and dirty process of removing the whole mess.

The beautiful, and quiet anchorage of Liscia, was thus filled with the sounds of sawing, cussing, and splashing water. Our troubles had ended with a silent row to shore, and a loud thud of a burden being thrown away. There was a quick celebration of the two happiest sailors, having finally rid themselves of the burden of carting around their excrement.

"I hated that toilet. Since we had rid ourselves of the holding tank and macerator, it is a seat, and nothing else. (Later we bought a composting toilet.) Every time I would try to pump the toilet, it would do one of two things, or both, whatever it felt like doing to me at that moment.

Number one: It would back flush and explode all over the place, including on me. I learned to close the lid, while flushing, to avoid the water splashing on my feet. It always ended with a bottle

of bleach and me, facing the issue of cleaning the mess.

And number two: It would flush with one swift pull of the lever, and all would be well. Later, though, as I would decide to brush my teeth, I'd smell the whole lot sitting in the toilet. It would slowly leak back into the bowl.

Those problems had finally been solved with one night, a trash can, and a port-o-toilet."
–Diary Entry, May 30, 2011

LA MADDALENA ISLANDS, SARDINIA

Pete and I bought our park passes for the Maddalena Islands with a fresh new toilet system. We spent two weeks cruising around the wind worn islands, and tied onto Park Authority mooring buoys.

Norna, during this time, did not have an electric windlass, the windlass we had was old and antiquated. One single link of chain was painstakingly winched in at a time. If depth was factored in, pulling in 100 feet of chain, with a 65 pound CQR, in 40 feet of depth, made for backbreaking work. Being able to tie Norna to a mooring, to say the least, was worth every penny.

BONIFACIO ,CORSICA

After our vacation from anchoring, we motor sailed into Bonifacio, Corsica - about a five-hour ride - and anchored with lines tied to the rocky shore.

Bonifacio was an amazing place to see. The sheer white cliffs cut a natural harbor, while a walled town was set high on the cliffs above.

The land was naturally carved by the wind. This carve was probably from the Mistrals that blew constantly from the Gulfe Du Lion. The harbor formed into a long tunnel, and a deep cut into the side of the mountain. The cliffs were straight up and narrow, giving the occupants above an advantage against pirates and intruders. Because their town was set high on the mountain sides, they could throw rocks and boulders down to protect themselves.

Chapter Twenty

Ghost Light
-Balearic Islands and Gibraltar

"It was now June and time for us to start heading out of the Mediterranean.

We were told from people we met along the way that 'It is easier getting into the Mediterranean than getting out'. We wanted to make sure there was enough time to arrive at the neck of Gibraltar, as September was only three months away.

We motored over to the Balearics during a calm in the weather. There was no wind. This was the only way to make our getaway from Sardinia without wind hard on the nose. We knew we had about a two and a half day passage to the Balearics. We wanted to land in Mahon on the southeast side of Menorca (Later Minorca or 'Minor Island').
–Diary Entry June 18, 2011

Pete and I endured two days of motoring, from Sardinia to Menorca on calm, flat seas. We were glad that we had calm weather, and made the passage without any adversity, except we worried we would not have enough fuel. We needed to be able to motor into a calm protected bay upon arrival, and with no wind on the horizon, we were unsure of how much farther we

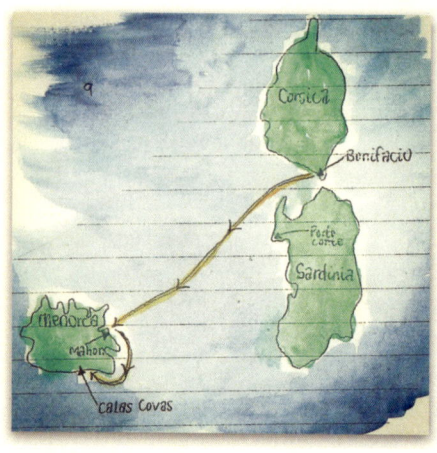

could go. On a positive note, we had the honor of watching a lunar eclipse in the calm Mediterranean Sea. The moon was red and it's bright rays glowed in the water, making it look like a rose necklace. Because of the glassy surface, Norna motored through a reflection of outer space, as the stars mirrored brightly against the dark sky. We waited for the winds arrival, gliding slowly along.

As the lunar eclipse passed, the wind picked up in a favorable direction, and we caught a ride to the Balearic Island of Menorca.

MENORCA, MALLORCA, AND IBIZA, BALEARIC ISLANDS

Pete and I anchored Norna at a few calas (or coves) around the south side of Menorca. My favorite cala was called Cala Covas (or Cove of Caves). The cala had many caves which use to be inhabited by hippies, (which had been run off) and turned into a park. It was deserted during the night, with only the beeping of a nightjar.

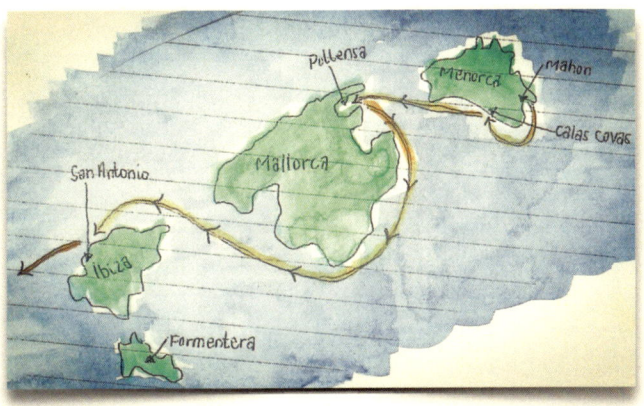

There were barely any tides in the Mediterranean Sea. Without tides, many boats could tie the stern to a rock, anchor off the bow, and not worry about drifting off hours later. This was, as I learned, called Mediterranean Moor (or Docking). This allowed several boats to fit in a small area.

Our arrival with Norna into the tight little Cala Covas must have been quite a sight. With Norna being a beamy 12 feet, and a 27 foot yardarm hanging over aloft, there were many wide eyed sailors. Several of them ran to the decks of their boats, putting out fenders, and watching with their mouths open. We motored next to our neighbor, with room to spare in the sardine space available. Pete backed Norna in, and tied the stern to a rock. We surprised ourselves of how smoothly this process went. Could we have pulled this off so smoothly next go around? Beginners luck, we guessed.

After exploring Menorca, and its several beautiful calas, we sailed to Porto Pollenca in Mallorca. We sailed alongside two American cruisers, named Sam and Bill, on a sailing boat called "Blue Banana." They had sailed together for several years from California, through the Pacific, and into the Med. They called us the friendly pirates, as Norna semi-resembled a pirate ship.

One breezy morning, in the wide bay of Pollenca, Sam and Bill decided to go for a sail on Blue Banana. We followed with Norna as the bay was a nice big bay to sail in. As Pete and I were sailing to the other side of the bay, we watched the wind dance around in circles.

This was not an uncommon thing in the Mediterranean. Within a matter of minutes, the wind would change its mind from blowing a nice light southwest 5-10 knots, to blowing a ripping 25-40 out of the northeast. I learned why the winds were named, though I had better names for most of them.

Norna sailed powerfully through this heavy 40 knot bipolar wind. Her sails stretched, and she heeled farther over than I had felt before. At first, Pete and I stood with our mouths open. Norna was handling this heavy wind very well, maybe too well. We worried we'd break something. Pete and I dropped Norna's outer jib, and pointed into the howling wind to reef her main. Without the outer jib hoisted, we could reef our main, back our inner jib, and hove to. Right at this moment when Pete and I finished our reef, the wind slowed enough for us to continue sailing comfortably. We anchored with Blue Banana, in a safe spot, on the other side of the bay.

Sam and Bill introduced us to a net called The Magellan Net (Mag Net) on the Single Side Band Radio or SSB. The SSB radio is a great tool for many sailors, and commercial ships, to speak over long distances. The Mag Net was a group of many cruisers who called in to catch up on local information of ports of call. It had followed through the Med, and later down through the Canaries, across the Atlantic. We met most of the cruisers on this net by both planned meetings, and by chance.

Thanks to Sam and Bill on Blue Banana, we had found a great way to keep in touch with a cruising community. Sadly, the following year, Sam on Blue Banana passed from cancer. She had bravely battled this disease during her cruise around the world. We will forever remember her as our friend, and positive sailor. Sail on Sam.

Through the Mag Net, we met an Australian couple on "Just Jane" named Jo and Arnie. This couple was ready to get out of the Mediterranean, and head down to the Canaries. Pete and I needed the motivation to do so, as well. We loved the Med for its beauty and history, but we had to take advantage of the winds.

Norna quickly cruised alongside Just Jane through Mallorca and Ibiza. The season was coming into full circle, "time and tide waited for no man."

CARTEGENA AND THE MAR MENOR
- with Just Jane

After cruising alongside with Jo and Arnie on Just Jane, we landed Cartegena on the mainland of Spain, in the Mediterranean Sea. Pete and I were anxious about not being able to afford the dockage in Cartagena (which was supposedly a good deal in the Med). Just as we were contemplating moving on, a man walked over to us and invited us to a wooden boat festival. This festival was in an inland sea just to the north of Cartagena, called the Mar Menor. We said our goodbyes to Jo and Arnie in Cartagena and sailed over to the festival.

We were invited to the Mar Menor for a week's free dockage, to be a part of a regatta. During the festival, Norna sailed far behind two 1900 era Fifes in a match race. We took many pictures of these beautiful sailing wooden boats. Pete was also invited to sail on Hispania, a 1909 Fife rebuilt for the King of Spain's grandson.

GIBRALTAR

August 13, 2011, after our week ended at the inland sea, we were really lucky; there was a good week of wind blowing the way we needed out of the Mediterranean. Pete and I gladly raised Norna's sails and set our course for Gibraltar, which we had missed on the trip in.

On our sail through the Straits of Gibraltar, the wind was in a steady light direction, and we had set our two square sails. These sails could be dangerous during some situations because they hang all the way to the deck. This can make for limited maneuverability, and visibility.

Pete and I decided it best to sail overnight, and arrive at the mouth of Gibraltar during the daytime. The winds were light, and directly

behind us, so we felt comfortable in leaving our square sails up during the night.

Because we were tired, we had failed to pay attention to the strength of the wind. It had gradually built to a howling 25 knots, and the waves became short and choppy. We suddenly had a scary, and dangerous situation on our hands.

We could not drop the square sails while sailing downwind. It would be a squirrelly situation, as the sails could fall into the water. Norna was surfing down waves; to have a sail for her to run over, would triple the complication. We could not turn Norna upwind, as the sails could backwind and possibly take the mast with them. We were stuck with square sails billowing out, like strong moth wings, for the time being. We felt the boat zig zag off the stern and considered putting a line out the back to straighten Norna out.

To compound the situation, Pete noticed - way later than he should have - that there was a boat ahead.

Dead ahead.

The weird thing about this boat ahead of us, was that it was acting fairly erratically, like no one was aboard. Pete and I saw the green, red, and white navigational lights jump back and forth. This gave us no particular clue as to what its intentions were. The boat was also motoring into the wind and waves, and whoever was driving, was not giving way to us.

Pete and I turned on our bright deck light and called them on the VHF. I looked at the square sails, they were really stretching from the heavy wind and seas. We were going at a powerful pace, and dangerously in trouble. I knew at that moment, that we could not possibly drop the square sails in time to slow down. We were speeding downwind, racing toward this boat at a powerful pace.

Pete and I called in vain on the VHF, the boat was not giving way. I looked at the charts, and saw that there were no navigational dangers in our area. We peered into the misting seas, between the giant square sails, at the light of the ghost ship. I helplessly screamed into the noise of the angry sea. The light of the abandoned boat peered eerily through the waves ahead. As we barreled down upon him, I strained my eyes into the salty air, with tears streaming down my face. There was nothing we could do.

Norna barreled ahead, and as we sailed closer, to our unbelievable relief, we saw that we were going to be within 50 feet of this vessel. We could not make out a hull amongst the waves. I stared hard at the shape, and screamed to the erratic boat. Norna quickly sailed by, as it disappeared behind us. It had faded away just as quickly as it came to being.

I shakily looked behind Norna at the faint light, Pete took his first breath of relief from the encounter. As quickly as it all had come to be, it had left us. It had left us shaken and fearful.

We both stayed up the rest of the night, keeping a watch, until our arrival in Gibraltar that morning.

Chapter Twenty One
Land Anxiety
-The Canary Island Arrival

We stayed at Gibraltar for a few days and rested from our near collision. A few days later, we sailed north, to Chipiona, to see our friend who had helped us fix our broken rig months before, Fernando. During our stay in Chipiona, a strong, hot Lavante blew, that blew red dust from the sands off Africa. The red dust looked like rain. August 21, we left for the Canary Islands. We were on our way back home.

GRACIOSA, CANARY ISLANDS

Pete and I had a beautiful and relaxing five day sail from Chipiona, with our square sails flying. The feel of the rolling Atlantic swells was such a vast difference from the short, choppy swells in the Med. There was a long way of open ocean, and the swells were more predictable, I didn't even feel seasick.

We were ready to land in Graciosa, the Canarian Island just north of Lanzarote. We had 20 miles to go, which was around four more hours, before we landed in Graciosa.

It was dark, very dark.

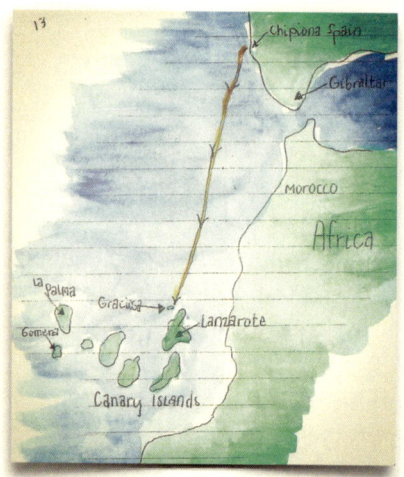

Pete had a tendency to panic when we arrived close to land. I didn't understand his fear, land had fresh food and showers to go to. Norna was right where we thought she was on our paper chart, I had plotted it from the GPS. Pete was not convinced, and continued to panic that land was nearby. He was worried about a particular unlit island to the port side of Norna, which we were miles away from. I was stressed from his panic, and stared at the radar for any sign of the offending island. I plotted Norna every 15 minutes on the chart, and called to Pete our coordinates.

After two hours of constant diligence, and being called down below to plot our course, I became weary, and mis-plotted Norna on the chart. I thought we were right next to this unlit island! Pete and I ran on deck, and dropped the square sails as quickly as we could get them down. We steered the boat to starboard, with the engine roaring. After several minutes, I went below to find that I had mis-plotted. I looked at the loud, roaring engine and back up at Pete. We *were* sailing peacefully. It would have been much faster, and nicer, than motoring with a roaring tractor engine in our ears.

I was tired and weary. With the added stress of Pete's discomfort of land nearby, the situation was not improving. I continued to try to calm his woes for the next two hours, as we endured an excruciatingly slow, and noisy approach into the marina of Graciosa.

Wearily, as we entered the marina port, we saw a light flashing onto a dock inside the harbor of Grasiosa. We made our way, and gathered our lines to throw to the man on the dock. As we pulled alongside, the man threw our lines back aboard. He pushed Norna off the dock and told us that we must go, there was no room.

"But this dock is open!" we called to the landlubber. He yelled to us to anchor at the beach.

"What beach?" We yelled to the insensitive port captain.

We did not know the area, our chart was not good for close up, I soon realized. I looked up into the sky and back out to the open water, that we were forced to go back to. The clouds blocked any sort of moonlight to decipher where to drop our hook. We circled the "full" harbor, and tried in vain to dock next to a fishing boat, which again turned us away. What dock does this?

I passed out. I could not take the stress of the situation anymore. For a few moments, I laid crumpled on the deck of Norna. I soon awoke refreshed, only to hear the sounds of Pete cussing at the marina. I remembered our situation again.

We never had a dock turn us away, even when there were open spaces. Granted, the weather was calm, and there were no waves. The problem was that we were weary from the stress of entering port, and had bad charts of the land. There were no lights on the island, or landmarks to navigate around, and we could have used the sleep.

We slowly motored out of the unfriendly harbor, to the sounds of waves hitting the beach. We felt blind. We could not see land anywhere and our chart was not helpful for depths. How interesting, I thought, we went four hours earlier worrying about an ominous unlit island; to anchoring in front of one.

Pete and I motored in closer to shore. I dropped our lead line to find the depths, as the pitch black darkness gave no clues. We wanted to anchor close in, so that we didn't have to drop the anchor in deep water. I worked feverishly to pull chain out of the bilge and ready our anchor. We were set up for cruise mode, with everything in its place.

As I was dropping the lead line, I started to hear the waves on the beach louder. We suddenly realized that we were nearly on the bottom! We backed up quickly and dropped the hook. With dock lines and fenders spread all over the deck, we went right to bed. I could not keep my eyes open any longer.

The next morning, after only two hours of sleep, we were awoken by an official boat. They knocked on our hull and told us we could not anchor at the spot we chose. What is wrong with this place? I thought. We were told to anchor at the next beach around the corner. Sleepily, we pulled up anchor, fired up the noisy Perkins, and settled into a deep anchorage next to other cruising boats.

"Surprisingly, Graciosa turned out to be one of our favorite stops after the anger wore off. Meanwhile, Pete and I had a long talk about his fear of arriving to land. He explained to me how he

had sailed his boat up to Michigan
and Canada, from Florida, when he
was 19 years old. He did not have
GPS and navigated land by sight.
He promised me that he would not
freak out with land nearby
anymore. We settled into a routine
of docking around the islands of
the Canaries, as anchoring proved
rough."
–Diary Entry
August 27

We wandered the black sand beaches of
Graciosa, and swam under a blown volcano.
There were no trees on this rugged island. The
few houses near the harbor were built on sand,
with sandy roads that few cars drove on. I
thought of the Wild West, with dusty roads, an
empty village, and heat rising off the stones.

The Seven Islands of the Canaries have
anchorages, some are exposed to open ocean,
and rock bottoms. Other than Graciosa, we did
not anchor at of any of them. We decided to dock
for the next three months, and enjoy the scenery,
before we headed back home across the Atlantic.
We wanted to have a safe place for Norna, so
that we could rent a car, and hike into the islands
a little more.

Chapter Twenty Two
Surfing Gone Wrong
-Lanzarote and La Gomera, Canary Islands

LANZAROTE

We sailed to a marina around the west side of Lanzarote, after hoisting up our anchor from the beautiful island of Graciosa, and docked. We decided to stay at this dock for only 20 days. The marina was extremely expensive and wanted to measure the length of our boat. Our 12 foot bowsprit, and our dingy davits made us much longer than 36 feet. We knew we were longer at most docks, but most docks did not mind this, and allowed for the payment of only 36 feet.

During our stay at the expensive dock in Lanzarote, we met a man named Lance. He was a local surfer and carpenter and worked locally around the docks. As he was walking with his bucket of woodworking tools, he looked at Norna, and set them down. He stood, rooted at his spot, examining our beautiful Danish built vessel. We greeted, and invited him aboard for a tour. As we talked in English, we learned that Lance was building a boat of his own. He told us he would take us to a local surf break, as he was a well-known surfer around the island.

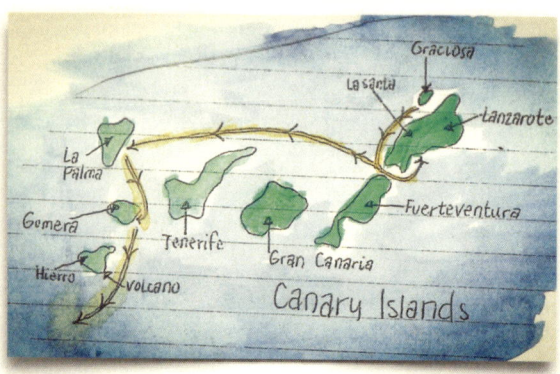

The following day, we went with him to a place called La Santa. "A world class wave", he told Pete and I, "it is like Pipeline in Hawaii". This should have been my first clue.

I had some experience surfing big 10 foot waves in Florida, what I did not realize, however, the vast difference a sand break would make. I was also out of shape from the lack of paddling. I had not built my back muscles up for surfing.

As we stood on the sea wall of the little town of La Santa, I looked down on the beautiful blue-green curls. The shore was overflowing with slimy, dark lava rocks. I decided I was going to give a rock break a try. Boy, was I lucky to have lived.

Pete and I walked over to an inlet, where fishing boats were motoring in and out of. I looked to my left and could see the break we were going to paddle into, they looked smaller from above on the sea wall. First Pete jumped in, me confidently following, and we paddled over to the break. Our hair had not even gotten wet. Upon first comparison to Florida waves, I was pleased that this break was a point break. In Florida, sometimes in order to get to the lineup, surfers paddled straight through tiresome waves and whitewater.

Pete caught the first curl that rolled in. I cheered on, and sat with the other guys that were waiting for the next set. The rocks were inches below me. I looked into the clear water and could see jagged volcanic rocks, with sea urchin spines wiggling in the current between. I looked around me to the shore. I would be in trouble if I did not catch a wave back to the inlet, I thought. The "beach" was nothing but pointy lava rocks. No longer could I paddle in to the safety of a sandy shore, like Florida. I looked at the guys around me who were waiting for the next set of waves, they were looking out at the horizon.

It was then that I realized, rock waves peaked out of nowhere! The wave jacked out of the sea, all the surfers near me scrambled to get away from the peak.

I was in the wrong spot. There was nothing I could do. I paddled my hardest to duck dive through the peak of the wave, but did not get enough momentum. The wave tossed me over backwards.

For a second, as I was soaring over backwards in the air, I thought about someday getting a VW Bus to travel. I then found myself tossed every which way under the water. After all the commotion, I had to paddle to air. I swam to the surface as fast as I could, and caught a breath. I was in the danger zone. There was another set coming, and white water was roaring in like a train.

I looked at the worry in Lance's eyes, he knew I was in trouble. He swam by me and pushed me forward. Pete hollered for me to paddle faster. I could not paddle fast enough. I was again thrown through the air and crumpled into the surf.

I had just enough breath to hold, because the second time I came to air, I was panting very hard from lack of oxygen. I began to panic. I paddled to the safety of shore, but shore was rocks! There was no way I was going to paddle back out in the surf. It had scared me enough.

Lance and Pete swam into the rocks with me, and helped me onto shore. I shakily climbed over the dangerous teeth, slipping around spots, and humbly limped to dry land.

Pete and Lance gave each other a knowing look. Lance explained to me that I was lucky that the tide was just right for me to swim to the rocky shore. Usually the waves would break right onto the black rocks, right where I was gasping for air. I had a visualization of being tossed onto the hard jagged ground, and sucked under, to be tossed again. Pete and Lance swam back out into the surf. I dried myself off, and looked at a large bruise on my leg.

Pete, after surfing several hours came in with pains in his feet. We looked at his pads, where the pain was shooting, and found that each foot had 30 black sea urchin spines. (We later soaked Pete's feet in white vinegar. Slowly, over a couple months, we removed the spines from his poor feet.) I had pain, and headaches in my neck, maybe a bit of whiplash. I was alive and well, and really grateful to Pete and Lance for saving my life.

The following day, we went to another surf break Lance had told us about. Pete and I were both beat up from my life and death experience, but Pete couldn't help himself. He loved to surf big waves, and could not get enough. Me, on the other hand, took videos from shore. Lance told Pete that the waves were like Sunset, a big point break off the black rocks into the inlet. Inside the inlet, was a nice Waikiki break for the kids to surf on. Just right for me.

I watched Pete surf on the giant curls. They were even bigger than the point break in La Santa. I knew Pete was hurting on his feet from the urchins, but he came in after a few hours smiling from ear to ear. He sat on the black sand to watch me surf the inlet waves. I looked out to the small, fun waves that rolled over the rocks below. The water was clear as air.

I couldn't believe it, but I paddled out. I could not focus on the Waikiki waves as I swam. I thought of my time spent on the beaches of St. Augustine. Every morning, I woke up and paddled out into the breaking waves to surf. I felt at home by the ocean shore. I remembered feeling troubled that I had moved away from the sounds of the ocean, when I bought Happy; but found Happiness in finding a home. Had I been too confident at La Santa? I had learned my limits, that's for sure. Interesting, I thought, how just a few years before, I couldn't have imagined being afraid to surf.

I arrived at the lineup on my paddle in the Waikiki waves, and was too afraid from my first encounter, to ride one single curl. The Pipeline break at La Santa had scared me; little did I know it would be a few years before I could bring up enough courage to surf again.

A few days later, Lance walked Pete and I inside of a blown volcano. It was a neat experience to meditate in the extreme quietness.There were no birds, no rustling trees, and not a single sound of cars, or people. Being inside this blown volcano was similar to the whole island of Lanzarote, like being on the moon. The terrain was rough and there were no natural trees. Along the landscape of this planet-like island were volcanoes that had erupted and covered up entire towns. Just hiking by foot proved to be too rough. The only smooth paths were the roads, cleared from the volcanic rocks and ash.

Pete and walked around a meditation circle in the center of the blown volcano with Lance. I felt a sense of relief while standing in this volcano. The noiselessness was somehow calming amongst the vast openness. I sat in the meditation circle. It was formed by several stranded rocks lying about, and was positioned directly in the middle. The sun shone down warmly onto the dark sand below. I thought about all the noise on a sailboat, and realized how noisy sailing was. The water slapped on the hull as Norna plowed along, cups clanged in the cupboard as she rolled, and the sails tugged and stretched as while the wind blew her. I meditated about surviving La Santa. I thought about our journey ahead. Pete and I had another crossing to complete in a few months, on our way to the Caribbean. I prayed for a safe journey for Pete and I, and said my goodbyes to Lanzarote.

LA PALMA

Pete and I sailed to La Palma, 250 miles to the West. This island was a total opposite experience from the barrenness of Lanzarote's volcanic lands.

La Palma, on the far west side of the Canary Island chain, was a stunningly beautiful Island. It was covered with large green forests and beautiful, vast views. There were giant ferns as tall as people, and beautiful Laurel Forests, that had endless trails and fresh air. The Island of La Palma was a biosphere, and rightly so. It was complete with volcanoes (which meant black sand beaches), forests, giant mountains, and reefs. Pete and I could smell the flowers from 10 miles out, upon our arrival.

We had heard a lot of talk about the side of La Palma sliding off into the Atlantic, and causing a giant tidal wave to the whole east coast of America. It was predicted to happen someday, but we found many skeptics on this issue, and enjoyed the island no matter.

La Palma was one of our favorite places in the Canaries. We docked Norna for a month. We spent this time hiking in the beautiful forests, walking down steep mountain sides, and exploring the giant prehistoric ferns that towered above our heads like dinosaurs.

LA GOMERA

In October, we sailed over to La Gomera, an island south of La Palma. Gomera was a small, mellow island, with beautiful hikes and green forests, very similar to La Palma.

We had decided to stay at the dock in La Gomera to prepare ourselves, and Norna, for the long sail across the Atlantic. During our stay, we met brave souls who were preparing to row across, on the same voyage we were preparing to take on Norna. We were docked next to the whole fleet of 11 rowboats.

A few weeks later, while we were docked at Gomera, Pete and I heard of an underwater volcano that was erupting on the southern tip of an island to the south, called El Hierro. We had planned to sail to this island, and stay at the very area of the erupting volcano! How amazing that we had planned to stay at Gomera instead!

While staying at the dock in the beautiful island of Gomera, we met a couple named Sue and Andy aboard Spruce. Sue and Andy were preparing to head across the Atlantic, as well.

Accidental Sailor Girl

Sue was a teacher who played flute beautifully. She was also practicing her classical guitar, while her husband Andy played the saxophone. They had decided to sail across the Atlantic, through the Caribbean and Panama, to the Pacific. We had talked with Sue and Andy on the SSB Mag Net, and knew we would be splitting off in separate directions after the Atlantic crossing. There were many days where we all would gather to play music, and hike around the beautiful island.

One afternoon, we all decided to go snorkeling by a semi-nudist beach. Pete and I had been to several nudist beaches in Spain, and by this time, had become accustomed to this normal practice. We even had spoken, on several occasions, how it would be nice to have the same practice in our own country.

While we were entering the water from this beach, I saw that there were several nude locals, and tourists, laying along the black sand beach, like birds. Sue, Andy, Pete and I decided to stay clothed as we set off, looking like funny platypus, with our snorkel gear and fins, into the blue water. We busily set out to the undersea adventures of fish. Sue and I snorkeled together, while Pete and Andy went off their way.

Sue and I came to the surface after snorkeling over an hour, at a safe distance from the boys. We stayed above the water talking about the many colors and types of fish, and were distracted by a very tan, fully naked man wading in the water, about waist high. Upon gazing, we watched Pete's snorkel lazily floating close by the bronze man. We giggled to each other as we watched Pete's snorkel, bob up and down in the current. He was casually swimming beside the waist-deep man, totally oblivious.

Pete, then noticing, suddenly stopped swimming, and raised his head out of the water in front of the naked man. He turned to Sue and I, as we were laughing hysterically at the entire scene. Sue and I still get a little laugh at this every once and a while.

Chapter Twenty Three
Sailing Back Home
  -The Trade Winds

"We left on November 29, and sailed for 25 days to the island of Grenada in the West Indies Caribbean Chain. We arrived two days before Christmas. Our next plans were to sail up through the Windward Islands, which would make for a hard beat to the

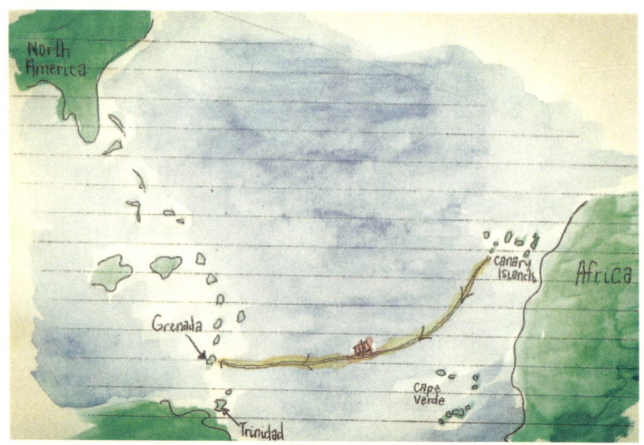

**Leewards. We would sail to the
Virgin Islands, and sail to the
Bahamas before May. We wanted
to have a little time to spend in the
Bahamas before our trip back to
Florida. We had four months."
– Diary Entry
December 23, 2011**

On the Crossing to Grenada, I had a sore
throat, and a cough that lasted the whole of the
journey. This worried me, I didn't want to get sick
offshore. We passed by El Hierro, on the most
southern of the Canary Islands, at a wide angle.
The active volcano was exploding. It had
breached the surface, and sent rocks high into

the air. We later heard of a new island that was formed.

Norna had her square sails flying for 15 days straight, without touching them. There were only a few times we adjusted for different angles of the wind. My minor seasickness only lasted one day, and I felt rested for most of the trip. I finally felt that I had somehow gotten over seasickness. I discovered that as long as I ate, and was not nervous, I was fine.

Pete caught a mahi mahi and a blue fin tuna. We had a few good happy meals with fresh vegetables that seemed to last much longer on the trip back home.

I had provisioned us way better on the second crossing. I had learned a few tricks to keeping fruits and vegetables longer. I also did not bring bananas, and avoided raw meat. I bought a huge salted leg of lamb that we carved off of instead. I bought several hearty vegetables that I could cut up and put in the pressure cooker for soup, such as cabbage and potatoes. I felt more confident in the boat, and my ability to navigate. Pete and I were happy to be heading back across on our way home. I learned from our first trip across the Atlantic, that not only was the crossing for the adventure of seeing new lands, but also the satisfaction of arriving safely back home.

I had a lot of time to think about how much I learned in two years' time, during the 25 days of Trade Winds. Throughout all of our passages, I had become so wrapped in ensuring we were navigating correctly, that I had not taken the time to look back. I had come a long way.

I thought of my eagerness to learn from Scottie, and couldn't wait to get back and see him again. I thought of the first time I had even stepped onto a sailboat and learned that there was another lifestyle. I thought of Happy and Bipolar, and laughed at the thought of when I had been given the job of untangling rope at Sailors Exchange in St. Augustine. My thoughts were soon stopped, as I heard Pete yelling for me to grab a hammer.

Pete decided it best to check our rudder, to ensure all was well on our steering. He discovered that the pin in the top gudgeon had worked its way out of its socket, and was precariously ready to fall off into the deep waters below.

I ran below decks, in the rolling seas, up forward to the focsle; and resurfaced outside with the hammer. I watched Pete adjust the tiller to turn back into the lineup of the pin to fit to the gudgeon. He then quickly tapped it into place. I was grateful to Pete for checking our steering system, and found that it did not move the remainder of the trip. It was times like this that reminded me to check on everything while sailing, even during a daydream.

Seventeen days out across the Atlantic, a low fell into the trade winds, and turned the wind on our nose. We headed south, to the longitude of Grenada to avoid this low, and for a week, began experiencing light winds. For a week, Pete and I sat, longingly looking into the blue ocean swells. On a positive note, we were in a current, because even with light winds behind us, we were still moving in the right direction. This was a great comfort in knowing this. We felt we were moving nowhere, but saw otherwise on our charts.

A few days out from land, as we became closer to the convergence zone, squalls arrived alongside frontal clouds. We did not know what awaited us on the other side of the ominous grey mist ahead, and when we spotted the squalls, this warned us to reef and batten down the hatches. Sometimes this frontal boundary brought no wind at all, and we were left with a boat ready for heavy weather.

Pete and I, however, did endure a few squalls where the wind had picked up heavier.

We would run Norna with the direction for a few minutes, until it blew itself out. We did not have to worry about sea room, so if we needed to go the wrong direction, we knew we had time to make it up. There were a few nights we stayed up all night on our watches, constantly adjusting for the angle of the wind. These nights became especially tiring, as they required all our attention and stamina.

"I had a rough time trying to cook dinner tonight. Pete and I had thought we did a good job of preparing for the crossing, to make cooking easier. We had tried everything, from plate holders, ready made meals, to making sure the tools to cook with were easily accessible. For the past 48 hours, it had been stormy and squally, which required every bit of stamina we had, to keep Norna with the wind.

We did not catch a fish this particular day, so I offered to make pot pie for dinner. The pot pies were in a can, and in theory, all that would be needed was, obviously, a can opener. Once the pies were in the oven, we would wait a half-hour, and voila, we

would have a cooked meal.
Sounds easy right?

Well, (eh hem) everything that could go wrong, went wrong. I went down below to the rocking belly of Norna. The kitchen was pitching in the rolling seas. This constantly required bracing myself on anything solid, while having my hands completely full. Items that were not screwed down, such as cans, spoons, forks, and lids, required hands, arms, legs, and teeth.

I attempted to open the can of pot pie, and immediately had to call for backup. The lid wouldn't open as it fought the can opener stubbornly, and we were forced to peel half the can lid. Doing this delicate operation while riding a bucking sailboat, was no small feat, believe me. Pete's pot pie decided to cooperate. Typical, I thought. Next, the stove wouldn't light. I held onto the bucking gimbaled stove, while Pete stuck his head inside, with a match to light it. We also were doing this balancing act while holding the pies. Well, the law of gravity happened, and my pie landed with a thud, jelly side down.

Once the pies were safely nestled in their cocoon of oven, we kept an eye on them. The gimbaled stove rocked in the rolling seas, and splattered juice all over the inside. I decided on 15 minute intervals of keeping an eye on the stove. Whomever was not stove watching, was squall watching, which required adjusting Norna to any changes of wind direction.

It was my turn to surface for air, while Pete was to go below. While I went into the cockpit, clipped into my harness, and watched for weather, Pete decided to open the port above the stove. It *was* hot with the oven on. Minutes later, I saw a green wave curl over the bulwarks and slap onto the cabin side. This wave had splashed into

the port, extinguishing the flame in the stove. This, of course, stopped the cooking process. Pete and I looked at each other in disbelief. Half warm pies was on the menu. Thank you, and your welcome."
–Diary Entry
December 12th, 2011

The heavy rain was very difficult the last week of our Atlantic Crossing. Norna's aft cabin was beginning to rot, we had not noticed this problem, until seeing how bad it leaked. (Pete later replaced this rotten lumber with heart pine). Norna, being a wood boat, required much attention to the seams in the decks. If the sun beat on its dry timbers, the tar barrier to our dry bunks below, would crack. This allowed for the sea to dump its wet substance all over our interior.

We decided it best to sleep in the forward cabin, which made for a more difficult stay. We had two bunks up forward, which had no lee cloths. One bunk was soaking wet from the pounding of the seas, so really, we had one bunk up forward with no lee cloth. Pete and I, thus had one dry bunk between us. Whenever we would share the bunk, Pete would fall off with a thud.

Eventually, we both slept on the floor, underneath the center table. It was the driest place aboard.

We had a couple waves break into the cockpit, both of which I was outside for, and both times I was clipped in. I was very glad to have clipped in my safety harness. The heavy rolling seas were like a fire hydrant, pushing hundreds of gallons over our bulwarks.

One wave curled, sneakily, from behind Norna. Its emerald green crest came over the aft side, exploded into the cockpit, and drenched me down through my rain gear. I was swept off my feet. I held onto the hatchway with both hands, as my legs served me no purpose. I screamed for Pete. The wave then broke into the hatch, down into the galley below. The white water rushed over the side of the boat, and Norna rocked violently to the noisy waves behind her. Pete awoke immediately to my screams, and came running after me. He broke every table and pot holder in his path. I stood in the cockpit, drenched like a rat. The worst was over. I hoped.

I learned that the North Atlantic crossing had much wider set waves, while the southern crossing was much choppier and wind driven. I was grateful of the kindness of the ocean, and absorbed the beauty in everything I could see. Even though the last week of our crossing had some incidents, Pete and I were thankful to arrive safe. I realized my respect for the ocean more than ever, I am forever grateful.

Chapter Twenty Four
Kick Em' Jenny
-Grenada to Carriacou, West Indies

GRENADA AND CARRIACOU

We arrived, after 25 days at sea, in Prickly Bay, Grenada. We heard the sounds of birds, the smell of spices, and was greeted by three magnificent things. First was a magnificent frigate bird, it flew about in circles, curiously looking down on Norna. Second was Sue, aboard Spruce, smiling happily at us, as she circled Norna in her dingy. Third was Andy, sitting next to Sue, smiling, and pointing at the frigate. They invited us for a fresh home cooked meal on Spruce. Just what we needed.

"We stayed in Grenada for a month. We provisioned, fixed a few things, and soon decided to head north to Carriacou. I had another lesson to learn."
-Diary Entry

Pete and I were heading to Carriacou, an island just 40 miles to the north. I decided to leave on a Saturday, instead of a Friday. The fear of leaving on a Friday is a sailor superstition that something will go wrong. The problem with going north to Carriacou was that the wind was not in our favor. We knew the winds *were* unfavorable, but we did not know how rough of a trip we would have, past the headland. The trade winds constantly blew across the Atlantic into the sea between Grenada and Carriacou. This made heavy currents, and a hard beat to windward, hence the name Windward Islands.

Pete and I left at three in the morning on Saturday, so that we would arrive during the daytime in Tyrrel Bay, on the island of Carriacou. To navigate the reefs of the Caribbean required daylight, so arriving at night subjected us to any dangers of running aground. Many guides warn of waiting outside of entrances until day.

Because I was being superstitious of leaving on a Friday, Norna was beating into heavy winds and seas, that the day before did not have. We sailed 24 hours over only 40 miles, in rough seas and strong northeast winds. We were pushed farther and farther out into the Caribbean Sea. Pete kept mumbling to himself that we were not going to make it to Carriacou. He mentioned that we should turn with the wind, and head to the Virgin Islands, about a five-day sail away.

I became very seasick, the most seasick I had ever been. I was scared from the beating of the waves and Pete's mumbling. I was not used to beating to windward, as most every trip we had been on was a downwind run. This left me so seasick I was debilitated. I could not feel my

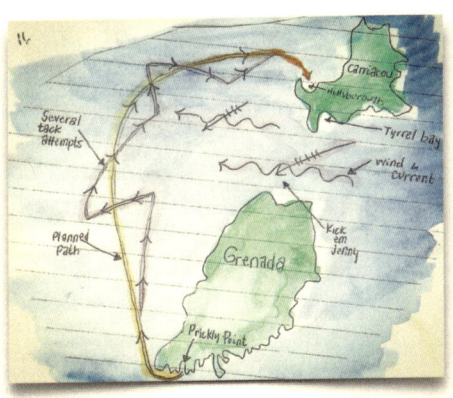

hands and feet, felt tingling in my mouth, and was to the point where I could not move my hands. I was stiff and could do nothing but lie down, leaving Pete to fend for himself, in the heavy seas and wind.

I knew Pete was in danger of sailing Norna by himself. I knew we had to get to land no matter what we did. I talked to myself, battered my fear, and soon found that I could sit up. I worked myself out of the debilitating stiffness and could finally help Pete. I fought my seasickness, something inside me told me not to be afraid. I knew my prayers were heard. We were going to make it.

Pete and I arrived at night in Hillsborough Bay (instead of Tyrell Bay). I was exhausted and weak, and could not read the chart correctly to know how to enter the bay. I actually held the chart upside down. The entrance, to my relief, was straightforward. Upon arrival, we dropped our anchor, dragged, and caught hold on the bottom.

We awoke a few hours later and made breakfast. Neither of us could eat very well, the boat was rocking and rolling uncontrollably. I looked around the anchorage. We were very open to a north swell. Pete decided we had to move around to Tyrrel Bay, a more protected place to rest.

Pete pulled up the anchor, and soon we were floating off the ground. Norna drifted backward and suddenly made a giant lurch. Had she run aground? We motored forward. The anchor chain pulled tighter, and Norna jerked over waves. We lurched in a weird way. What was going on? The anchor chain was tugging and straining the bow roller. Pete ran up forward.

The weight of the boat, and the taut chain, was ripping the roller out!

Pete ran up forward to the gypsy handle on the windlass. I could see him straining, trying to loosen the chain. Just as he was doing so, the roller ripped off the stem. I watched as the chain links skipped off the gypsy on the windlass, and the handle leap up and hit Pete square in the head!

I put the motor in neutral and ran up forward. Pete looked dazed. Blood ran down his nose and dripped in the wind. As it fell, it was thrown wherever the wind took it. I looked around the anchorage. The wind was gusting 25 to 30 knots!

We were in a dangerous situation. The bow roller was gone. The chain was violently tugging on our bare boat. We had no way of lifting the anchor. Pete took his shirt off and covered his bleeding head. I ran down below to call for help on VHF.

"This is the sailing vessel Norna, we have caught on something in the bottom and cannot get the anchor up, is there anyone that has a boat that can help us?"

I got a reply. "We have only a small dinghy and cannot help you. We *are* on the dock and there are some fishermen here that can help. Do you want me to send them over? They have a bigger boat."

A few minutes later a fishing boat came. Pete had cut our chain in half and linked the two spans of chain together with a shackle. He had done so months before this incident. I thanked our lucky stars, and watched Pete unshackle the two spans. He tied a giant fender to the end, and threw the whole mess overboard. We were free!

Pete dove in the water while I drove around in circles in the harbor. A half hour passed and I noticed that the ball and chain were aboard the fishing boat. Pete was aboard, smiling, his head wound beginning to swell. The fishing boat drove over to me.

"Kourtney, the anchor was hooked on a giant 15 foot fisherman anchor!" Pete shouted.

"No! Did you get it back?"

"I had to dive 12 feet and unhook it, we got it back!"

We pulled the anchor onto the boat and thanked the fishermen. They told us they had trouble offshore too, and had run out of fuel. We were very thankful to have gotten our anchor back. It was our best anchor, a 65 pound CQR and about 200 feet of chain. This would all have been hooked to the giant fisherman anchor, 12 feet below.

We slowly made our way to Tyrrel Bay, having to wait out a rainstorm that included fog, and dropped our rescued anchor in the safe harbor. It was calm, and still. I listened quietly to the sound of roosters crowing and goat bells tinkling.

I looked at Pete's head. He was becoming a unicorn, but the cut was minimal. Because of the fear of concussion, Pete was not allowed to sleep. After 24 hours of travel, and going through the worst of anchor dramas, sleep was the one thing both of us wanted to do. For the next seven hours we laid awake, until finally our eyelids could not take the weight anymore.

Chapter Twenty Five
The Family Who Lived in an Almond Tree
-Windwards to Leewards, West Indies

"We sailed from Carriacou to the Tobago Keys, and swam with turtles. We heard from locals that this was an exceptionally windy year. The Christmas Trades didn't want to quit blowing. We sailed to Bequia and then to Dominica, our favorite island in the Caribbean. We then sailed straight to Virgin Gorda in the Virgin Islands and worked our way through to St. John and

the famous Coral Harbor. We then headed to
the Exumas, in the Bahamas. We wanted to
be in Florida the beginning of June."
– Diary
Entry May 2012

DOMINICA

We arrived in Dominica with hearts full of
gladness. We were finally out of the Windward
Islands! It was smooth sailing from here, I
thought. The wind would either be behind us, or
on our side the rest of the way.

We anchored safely in Portsmouth harbor on
the island of Dominica. After ensuring that we
had set anchor and had a good lunch, we rowed
to shore. It was always nice upon arrival to be
able to explore our new surroundings and stretch
our legs a bit.

We walked on the sandy beach and saw a
man with a walking stick. He looked wild and
wind-worn with a machete on his side. We
approached him and asked about his walking
stick. He began to smile. His walking stick was
made from a bay tree and had many twists and
bends. It had burn marks of symbols imprinted
into its bark, was finely oiled, and looked to be
worn on the handle, where he had used it for
many hikes.

His beard was beginning to dread into the
hair on his head. His dark dreads were curling

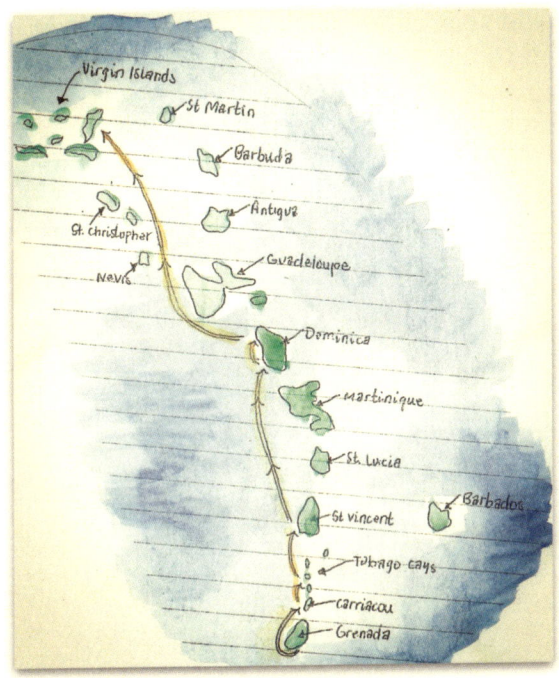

into themselves, and weaved into several layers of time. We learned his name was Dean and he lived in a treehouse. We asked him about the island, and he told us about the many waterfalls and places to hike and canoe. We thanked Dean, and walked along a path that led into a forest, along the mouth of Portsmouth Harbor.

Along the way, we met a woman who also had a machete on her side. She sported a walking stick of the same design, and was picking what we later learned to be cacao for her son. Her son was happily playing with a conch shell on the banks of the harbor.

We talked to her, as well, and learned that her name was Marva, she was Dean's wife. We talked with her a little while and told her we had arrived on our sailboat. We mentioned that we were thinking of staying a few days, and exploring her beautiful island.

Pete and I wandered back off into the forest. He grabbed my hand and we turned around. We walked back to Marva and helped her carry her basket of herbs and cacao to the treehouse. It was getting dark. We could not see the house in the almond tree that her family was living in, but could see a faint fire around the back. I was very interested in their lifestyle. What amazing people! I smelled rice and bread cooking. Marva thanked us for helping her and gave us bay leaves and wild lemons. We happily got back into the coconut to row home to Norna for the night.

Pete and I spent the next few nights finding food and washing laundry. I decided to wash my laundry on the boat by hand. It was easier to do a load a day, and hang it all to dry, than to drag the whole burden to shore. I learned that I could fill a bucket with salt water and laundry soap (biodegradable, of course) and after scrubbing, rinse twice. First, with salt water to rinse all the soap, and again with fresh, to eliminate all the salt. Our laundry came out clean every time.

A few nights later, we rowed the coconut onto the beach to see if we could find the family in the almond tree. We saw Dean chopping coconuts and pouring the juice into a calabash bowl for Marva. I looked in the almond tree and noticed the house was shaped as a boat. It looked to bend with the movement of the limbs, almost as though the house grew with it. Later, Dean explained to us that he had built his home so that when the wind blew, every wall of the home would move with the tree.

Marva looked up, noticed Pete and I, and called us over. She introduced us to her daughter and son, and walked us around the back of the almond tree to the campfire. As we walked under the tree, I saw several homemade pots, pans, coconuts, and calabash bowls. I looked into the fire and watched Dean push four full logs in a circle. The ends of each log faced into the hot coals, and began to glow with each flame. We all sat around the fire and watched the sun set. Dean pushed each log deeper into the coals, whenever the fire burned down.

Dean gathered some flour and water and began to knead dough, as his son and daughter sat around the fire next to us. Pete looked happily at me, as I knew he was thinking of Ava at home. We were missing her greatly at that moment. I watched the children take sticks and dig for earthworms. Dean looked around at the few houses on the beach and looked at us. He began to explain his lifestyle.

"See these houses around us?" He began to form the dough into little circles, and then poured coconut oil into a pan.

Pete and I looked around at our surroundings. We saw many palm trees and houses amongst them. Behind us, was a steady slope to a mountain, with a beautiful wet forest land. Dean continued his conversation as the bread began to fry in the pan.

"These houses will not be here when there is a hurricane. The wind and waves are going to wash them away. They will have no solid ground to stand on, except the mountains to run to." He took out the bread and cut a pocket into each. He placed them into a basket to cool. He then took the many gatherings that Marva had collected in the forest and began cutting up pieces of roots and herbs.

"But this almond tree has deep roots that cannot be washed away. It will be able to take the heavy winds and withstand the storm." He placed the cuttings into the pan to cook and sat next to his children.

Pete and I asked Dean about the many plants that he gathered. He explained to us about the many roots we could pick, and the edible flora and fauna to look for. He showed us how to boil various roots like potatoes, and explained how to make chocolate from cacao. The seeds from a cacao fruit was dried and mashed into paste. The flavor of chocolate was achieved by adding boiled sugarcane to taste.

Dean retrieved his water from the several waterfalls on Dominica, and could pick coconuts whenever he was thirsty. This was why he carried a machete, Dean explained. Whenever he was thirsty, he did not need to carry his water, he could climb a coconut tree to find it.

Marva came down to the fire and we watched as Dean stuffed his bread with the cut potato roots and herbs he told us about. We ate what Dean explained to us was called stuffed bakes. We were really glad to have met the family in an almond tree.

Pete and I decided to stay in Dominica longer. The beauty of both the island and the family we met, was exactly what we were looking for. Over the next few weeks we explored the many paths and forests. We swam at many waterfalls, and canoed in a mangrove river.

One morning, we watched as Dean made his special walking sticks. He burned a knife in the never ending fire and carved symbols and swirls in its bark. As Dean was carving into the walking sticks, a man walked into his home. He demanded rudely to buy one of the sticks. Dean explained to the man that they were not for sale, and the man walked away angry. Pete and I looked at Dean with surprise.

"This is not the first time this man has demanded to buy one of my walking sticks." Dean began to walk away from his fire. Pete and I followed, and watched as Dean began to climb a nearby palm tree.

"Are you thirsty?" Dean asked us as he began to climb.

"You don't have to climb for us, we can walk and get water from the restaurant up the way." We pleaded to him.

Dean smiled at us, and began climbing the tree. In no time, he was sitting on the top, chopping away at the stems of the coconuts. A giant bunch fell to the ground. Dean quickly scaled the tree to inspect the bunch. He picked through them and found that none were broken.

"That man also wanted to pay me to climb a palm tree for a coconut. He wanted it too much. I climbed the tree for him, and when they all had fallen, not one had water for him to drink. I could only hand him broken coconuts."

Dean picked up a freshly fallen coconut, and chopped it open for me to drink. When I was done, he chopped it in half for me to eat the meat. We collected all the coconuts, cleaned off all the shells, and took some home with us to drink. (These came in handy when we were offshore on our way to the Virgin Islands.)

Deans' girlfriend Marva invited me up in the treehouse. I saw that it was built like a boat. It was built around the tree, to be part of a living thing, and not to stamp it out. The wood they used was hand-carved and naturally oiled from coconut oil.

Pete and I became good friends with the family in the almond tree. Dean and Marva taught us to roast coconuts to make oil, and to make coconut milk with shavings. We carved calabash bowls, and had many home-cooked meals by campfire. Pete went through his hand tools and gave Dean any spare things he had, in return for the great friendship we were acquiring.

Dean looked like a magician, and as we got to know him better, we realized that he was living the magician's dream. He had taught us many lessons about being a steward of the earth.

Living life does not require the best job, or the most money. In fact, it is not about what many rasta people call "Babylon," (or the love of money.) Life is about food to eat and the shelter we choose to make for ourselves. It is about living off the land, and knowing how.

It was during our time in Dominica that we realized there was an alternative to life. It was for the living, not living to get ahead. It was as though our brains were rewired to another frame of life. That this was what life was for. We could be farmers, and build our homes, wherever this home was. Life was for learning, and what better than to learn of the seasons of food, and when to pick on what phase of the moon. To learn what could be eaten in the wild, and generally how to live simply.

Dean and his family were not living a life any harder than anyone else. In a way, it was better. Their comfort was compromised, and sometimes they had difficulties with what life threw at them, but they were no different. They understood what was important in life. When it all came down to the basics, after everything else was lost, eating and water are essential. If we could provide for ourselves, our shelter, and keep ourselves healthy, then that will keep the fire burning.

Pete and I left Dominica with our minds and bellies full. Our hearts were flowing with joy.

Dean brought us the walking sticks we watched him make, and we said our warm goodbyes to our amazing rasta family in a treehouse. They showed us a trail to follow in our lives, and a goal we always want to remember.

VIRGIN ISLANDS

"We sailed to the Virgin Islands, and worked our way through at a decent pace. Time was running short, we needed to sail to the Exumas before April. Norna had several beautiful sails around the crystal clear water of the Virgins. Everywhere we looked there were green mountain landscapes, surrounded by soft sandy shores. Whichever way the wind blew, we always had a beach to swim to. We loved St. John, it had many trails and natural campsites, and was mainly a state park. We also enjoyed Coral Bay, with all the friendly folk living on their sailboats. We could not fly Ava to see us in the Caribbean as we had planned. We missed her more than ever, and tried our best to stay positive. We moved north to the Turks and Caicos and stayed for a week during cloudy weather. The weather mirrored our mood. It was March, and the summer fronts from the north brought afternoon rains. We prepared our passage to Conception Island."

Chapter Twenty Six
So Close But Yet So Far
-Nassau, Bahamas

Pete and I traveled north to Conception Island with a plan. We knew we could bring Norna to the Caribbean again, and the next time we traveled for an extended time, Ava would hopefully want to come. Our arrival to Conception Island was magical. The sun burned the clouds, and the white sandy bottom glowed up at us. I looked up at the clearing sky and was stunned by the mirrored blue reflection glimmering up on Norna's hull. Pete looked at

me, and after anchoring, we dove into the clear water. He dove down and dug the anchor deeper into the sand, as I swam on the surface. We dropped the coconut down from the davits, rigged up the sail, and sailed to the bright white sandy beaches. Every direction we looked, the beach had no footprints. Someday, Ava is going to come with us here, I thought. I looked over at Pete, I knew he was thinking the same.

We stayed on Conception for a few days, and traveled north through the Exumas. It was nearing the end of April. Several of our friends from the Mag Net traveled along with Norna. We spent time snorkeling and exploring the mangroves of the picturesque islands. We traveled north to Nassau in the middle of May.

Once we arrived in Nassau Harbor, Pete an I knew we had a two-day sail to Florida. We were only two days away from home! It was then when we were struck with the most difficult problems we were to face during the entirety of our trip. We endured one more test before our arrival home.

We anchored Norna by the bridge in Nassau, and put two anchors down. We had to do so because boats around us also had two anchors. I remembered the Bahamian Moor

Scottie had shown me on Happy almost two years before.

While in Nassau, we provisioned and made ready for the last leg of our trip to Florida. Pete decided one morning to run the engine to check on a leak.

Perky was beginning to drip diesel fuel around the injector pump.

While Pete was working in the engine room, I sat outside putting food in bags and cleaning the cockpit for

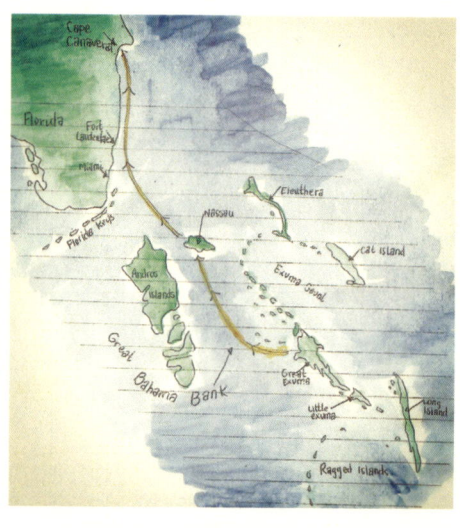

the arrival home. I was busy wiping salt water crystals off the dodger, when I heard the engine rev up higher. I ran to the throttle to rev Perky down. I figured Pete had accidentally hit something to throttle the engine up. Nothing happened. As I continued to shift the throttle, the engine continued to rev higher. Pete stuck his head out of the engine room. He yelled over the roar of Perky for me to throttle down. He saw that I was throttling the engine and nothing was happening. I looked at his confusion. What was happening?

The engine screamed as it revved up higher and higher. It began to blow white smoke out of the exhaust. It looked as though a rocket was shot into the back of our boat. By this time the engine was roaring! Perky went its full revolutions, shot back down to neutral, and revved higher again.

We were having a runaway diesel!

Pete screamed to me to shut it off. I pushed the button and nothing happened. Panic set in.

"It isn't shutting it off, pull the solenoid!" I screamed. Seconds later Pete emerged unsuccessful.

"What do we do?!" I screamed to Pete, I could see the panic in his eyes. He was scrambling for an answer. The sound of the engine exploding itself was enough for anyone to handle.

"Shut off the fuel" Pete screamed over the engine, and thus began his attempt at doing so. I screamed for help to nearby boats. I saw a friend we met on the Mag Net, Tony on Tactical

Directions, emerge out of his boat. He scrambled in his dinghy and came over as fast as he could.

Tony climbed aboard and saw our panic. I was begging him for an answer of how to stop our engine before it blew itself up.

"Let me think" he said twice as he looked down below. Pete's face was in the engine. The whole lot spewing antifreeze and water out of its breather. It was screaming as loud as an engine could be.

"I have a runaway engine!" Pete yelled to Tony, "I have to stop the fuel" he looked at me, "Kourtney, get in the dinghy and row away in case this thing catches fire."

I did as I was told. I ran to the coconut, and pulled it alongside Norna, several sailors nearby were getting in their dinghies to help. Suddenly, the engine stopped. All was quiet.

I realized the only sound I could hear was me screaming and crying. Without thinking I got in the dinghy and rowed around in my hysterics. I could hear Pete talk excitedly to Tony. I rowed back to hear Pete explaining how he had shut off the engine.

"I tried kinking the fuel hose, pulling the solenoid, and finally I found a straight slot screw driver to pull the fuel hose off the engine! Luckily it had gotten a bubble in the line! The air in the line shut it down!"

Minutes later, other boats in the harbor were arriving with their input.

"You should have put a book on the air breather!" "You have a faulty injector pump," many people were talking at once in all the excitement. Pete and I did nothing but look at each other. What were to do now?

We talked with many locals and decided that the injector pump must have been the culprit. This was where the leak was. I learned a lot about a diesel engine.The oil sump was filled with diesel, and this must have been what had caused the runaway. The diesel must have been leaking in from this faulty injector, and filling the oil sump. It must have filled up so much, that it overflowed and ran off the fuel in the pistons. The next problem was, where were we to find a person to fix our injector pump?

We decided it best to relax the rest of the day, or at least try to. My nerves were shot. I worried that because it had run away, rods could have bent, or internal damage was done. Would we be stuck in Nassau harbor for the season? Would we have to haul out and pull the engine? Would Perky run away again? Pete and I rested. He comforted me in my anxiety, as I fell asleep for the night. We were so close, but yet so far.

I dreamed I was in an elevator and it was running away. We were going up with a great amount of speed, and back down again. I woke up in a sweat.

I walked into the companionway and saw Pete making coffee and tea. I heard the Single Side Band radio crackling with the sound of local cruisers. I listened. There was a hurricane traveling up to Florida.

"Good time for a hurricane. We can't go anywhere right now anyway," he said to me. He saw my face and hugged me.

We sat and had our breakfast. When Pete heard his turn to ask a question on the net, he piped on the mic. He explained of our runaway engine, and asked if there was anyone in Nassau that could fix a leaking injector pump. There were many mixed replies. Some mentioned sending it to Miami. It would be a few weeks before the return. Pete and I knew this was not possible. Other replies were for us to talk to a mechanic. Injector pumps were only to be installed by a professional. This could be really expensive. Our hopes began to crash.

Suddenly, a man piped in. He mentioned about a boat that had a leaky injector pump 10 years ago. There was a man who fixed the pump. He was across the street from where Norna was anchored, in a car garage. The man was silent for a moment to jog his memory. He mentioned that an injector pump could be removed on a Perkins engine, as long as it wasn't turned over. Pete thanked the man on the net. After breakfast he set out to find this man in the shop across the street.

"I found him Kourtney! He told me how to pull the injector. He also said he would be willing to work on it in the next few days." Pete said as he was rowing to Norna in the coconut. I gave Pete a hug, once he boarded. I knew it would take a few days to delve into the motor, and pull it all apart. I was so grateful to have found a person to fix our pump!

Over the next few days, Tony on Tactical Directions and Pete had their heads in the engine. I was invited to have a girl's beach day with some friends around the anchorage. I was so grateful to have the opportunity to leave our situation, and go only a few miles, to a nice sandy beach.

Upon our return, Pete showed me the injector. It looked as though we had the diesel bug. There was a milky substance in the pump, and it looked to be in our fuel as well. Pete explained that we would need to pump the old fuel in a container, clean the tank, and put in new fuel. I sighed. That was not going to be an easy task.

Over the next few days, the boat became a wreck. Perky was in shambles, and we delivered our faulty injector pump. We pumped out the infected fuel into a 55 gallon drum, loaned to us from a local fisherman, and contemplated where we got the bad fuel from. Gibraltar? Somewhere in the Caribbean?

We cleaned the tanks, and the following morning delivered the entire vat back to the fisherman. As the days went by, we filled Norna back with fresh fuel, gave her an oil change, and gladly received our injector pump back.

Pete spent the following day reinstalling the pump. That evening, after a hard days work, Pete told me he was ready to start the engine. I was scared of Perky after the runaway, and ran up on the foredeck. I heard the engine fire up after a few attempts of bleeding the air. After minutes of running, Pete came out and shut it down.

"She is still filling the oil sump with diesel."

Pete and I sat sadly to dinner. We both went to bed with heavy hearts. Our engine was not fixed, and the injector pump was not the problem. What could it be?

The following morning, we heard the hurricane had stayed offshore and was heading to Bermuda. We needed to get Perky working. Was it a faulty lift pump? Was the antifreeze not bled? We tested both, and found them not to be so. Pete left me on the boat, as he went to bring the injector pump back. I sat aboard Norna thinking about how our engine could have run away again. I didn't know if I could handle two run-away engines in a matter of a week.

After several hours, Pete returned shaking his head.

"I told the man that the pump was still leaking. He told me it was packed with the diesel bug and he had cleaned it out." Pete made a motion with the injector pump, tipping it upside down. He explained to me, in the typical Caribbean accent, what the man said, "it wasn't leaking when I tipped it like this, mon."

I laughed a sigh of relief, the man did not replace the right seal and was going to take the pump back. Hopefully we would have a fixed pump the following day.

The next day came, and we feverishly put the engine back together. After I ran to the foredeck, Pete started the engine once more. It was making a terrible clanging noise at low RPMs. We both felt weak. Pete checked the sump, and found it not to be leaking anymore.

"It must have air in the lines somewhere, or a piston rod is just out of place" Pete explained after much coaxing for me. He revved the engine up higher. The clanking did one last bang and the engine was back to its normal purr.

"There, whatever it was has just fixed itself." Pete checked the water out the exhaust, all was fine. The temperature came up to heat and stayed at a normal temperature, the water and oil level staying constant. We finally, after two weeks had a "fixed" engine.

We picked up the pieces of Perky, with all the tools around, and stocked ourselves back up with food. We knew it was good that we had stayed in Nassau, we needed to to hide from the hurricane that followed our path up Florida. The weather was not good for going north, it was as though Perky stopped us.

We planned to arrive in Cape Canaveral, Florida and sail up to Titusville to meet up with Ava. We were going to be back in our home country in two days!

Pete went ashore to find some bilge diapers and I stayed aboard to clean the boat and tidy our tools. I noticed some black clouds to the north and told Pete to return before the black clouds came closer.

Ten minutes later, the wind picked up furiously and the tarps rattled the rigging. I heard loud cracks of thunder and lightning. This came way sooner than I had predicted. I immediately shut off the electronics and ran outside. I pulled in towels, and as I was folding them and putting them away, I saw a flash of lightning strike, big and heavy, behind the boat. It lifted the back of the boat with a wave, and the boat began to tug on our Bahamian Moor. Norna lurched and spun in circles. I looked outside. Was I in the middle of a waterspout? It was as if the day became night. I could not see land. The only thing I saw was a gloomy mast of my neighbor sailboat, through the porthole.

The lightning struck every two seconds and the wind blew furious and angry. I stuck my head outside. Norna was facing a different direction, in comparison to the boat next to me. I felt the boat lurch sideways, to a gust of what I could guess of more than 50 knots. I listened to the tarps rattle themselves loose and flap uncontrollably. I grabbed scissors and ran outside to cut loose the remainder of the tarps. The lightning struck all around, and I ran below completely soaked from rain.

I began to pray. The storm was not leaving after an hour. Each time I stuck my head to get my bearings, Norna was facing a different direction to the sailboat mast next to me.

I heard a loud crash on the bowsprit of the boat. I looked outside, to see that there was a boat dragged against us. It was drifting dangerously close to our yard arm. Many sailors forget to look up when coming up to Norna, and some have come close to hitting this extension.

There was nothing anyone could do at this moment. I was too afraid to start the engine, as we had just repaired it. To go outside during this storm, was too scary for me to handle after all the stress I had been through with the motor running away.

I watched the boat unstick from the bowsprit, drift past, missing our yard arm, and drag into my neighbor. I watched a man on deck, a single-hander, during all of the lightning and strong winds, trying to pull up his anchor with a manual windlass.

I saw hail, and heard what sounded like a train. I laid on the floor. The storm blew strong for two hours, and just as quickly as it came, I heard the rain and wind lighten up. I went outside to see the damage.

Norna dragged next to a Wharram Catamaran, close enough to hand them a cup of coffee. Our second anchor dragged, but our CQR held firm. I later wondered if the man who dragged, had caught our second anchor. I thought better of this, as Norna had spun in circles, and pulled hard on every axis.

I waited a half-hour for Pete to arrive on Norna, and he did not come. I called over to my neighbor. They were surprised that someone was aboard, as they saw no dinghy attached to Norna's hip.

My neighbor rowed over, and helped to move the dragged anchor. I soon became scared of what had become of Pete. Did he try to motor in the coconut during the storm? Did he get caught in the tornado, or waterspout?

I sat on the bow of Norna, staring at the shore Pete had left Norna to go to. Forty-five minutes later, Pete appeared in the distance. He explained to me that the coconut sunk. He said that the whole city flooded, and that he could not leave until after the wind lightened.

We both looked at each other and knew it was time to be home. We knew that we only had two days to arrive in Florida; two days until we saw Ava.

We had survived, and no matter what happened, we were going to have a happy ending.

Pete and I went to bed the night before our departure to Florida, with hearts full of happiness. We had endured some of the roughest times, at the edge of being so close to home. Norna had survived. We had survived! I found peace in knowing home was only two days away. We were going to make it now, and give Ava a much needed hug.

Chapter Twenty Seven
The Next Accidental Beginning
-Cape Canaveral, Florida

Pete and I had a very good sail to Cape Canaveral. The weather was calm, though we skirted small isolated thunderstorms. It was now the end of May. We had arrived back to Florida around the same time we had left.

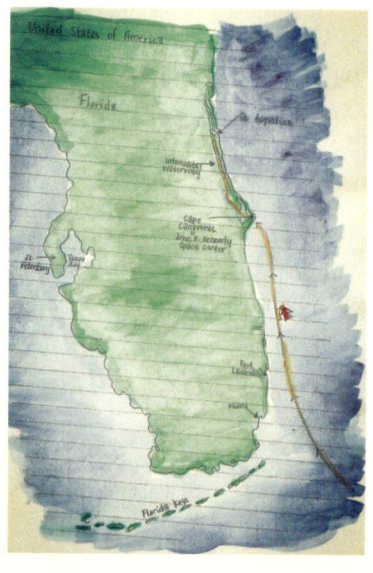

We watched land appear on the horizon. I smelled the warm breezes from land, which carried the scent of sunscreen. We docked Norna at a place that allowed us a shower, checked into customs. We spent the night, moved through a lock, and motored to Titusville.

Ava arrived in Titusville. Hugs were given, along with smiles, and stories. We had a lot to talk about. Ava travelled with us the rest of the trip to St. Augustine. Pete and I spent all our time with her, it was as if we had never left. We motored up to Marineland in a beautiful nature reserve, and had a flag raising party. We took Ava surfing, as the beach was across the street, and she began to learn mandolin.

During this time, we started to get back into finding work, and finding a nice place to rest for a while. We were surprised on how easy it was to become use to the land life again. Norna had served us well, we were home.

I had a life changing journey. There were a few times in our travels where I wanted to quit. I was ready to fly back and live on a farm. I had realized that I was not the same person I was when I left. I can safely say that I have a greater knowledge of the world. No matter where I am, I am home. I feel I have found peace from my past. I am always learning every step of the way.

During this time, I took a step back to think of the long two-year journey I had taken. I thought of all the effort I had taken to find my way to this journey, and thought of the lessons I had learned.

I learned patience, more patience than I could ever dream of. There were many times when we knew it would be another six hours before we got to land. There were times when we knew we could not go to the next port, because of weather, or broken parts.

I had learned acceptance. Sometimes, we had to turn around, and return back to a safe port. Sometimes, I had to accept when I was wrong on how to set a sail. I had to accept that I would not get to shore for a few days, due to a storm. Accept that, for a few days, I would be seasick, because the weather turned the waves into a washing machine.

I had learned to do without. All my zippers corroded, all my clothes had holes, and every piece of metal had rust. There were closet spaces used for something other than clothes, and money to be spent on ourselves, that was almost always changed into money spent on the boat.

So "what's next?"

I had a bucket list of things I wanted to do from childhood, and since this journey I had altered my idea. I had always wanted to travel cross country in a Volkswagen Bus. From looking at this poor world and the constant dilemma of gas and car fumes, I decided to change my tune a little. I decided after crossing the Atlantic Ocean, after living on solar and wind, and seeing the importance of water, that I would further my quest for being green.

Being on a sailboat, has taught me that the earth has a lot to offer in the way of energy. If this energy is used in a positive way, it can be beneficial to both us, and the environment. I decided that the best way to conquer this problem of getting stuck in the normal flow of traffic, is to go back to the roots.

My first bucket list of the nomadic life of a sailor, is to convert a Volkswagen Bus to run on propane, and begin little land travel. My second bucket list, is to take a horse and buggy across the country.

Watching old westerns I saw men on horseback, and in old wagons. I wondered if this could be attempted now?

Why not travel cross-country by horse and buggy? Take back roads, travel slowly, treat your horses well, and make your buggy a small camper van. Complete this with all that is needed for cross-country travel. I have seen a lot of the Atlantic and Europe and the Caribbean. The earth is so big! There is so much earth to see! If I could do one small step, work toward another new beginning, why not see some of my own land? Why not travel by horse and buggy?

Why not do so the way it was done in the past, just as sailors have done for hundreds of years?

The Beginning.

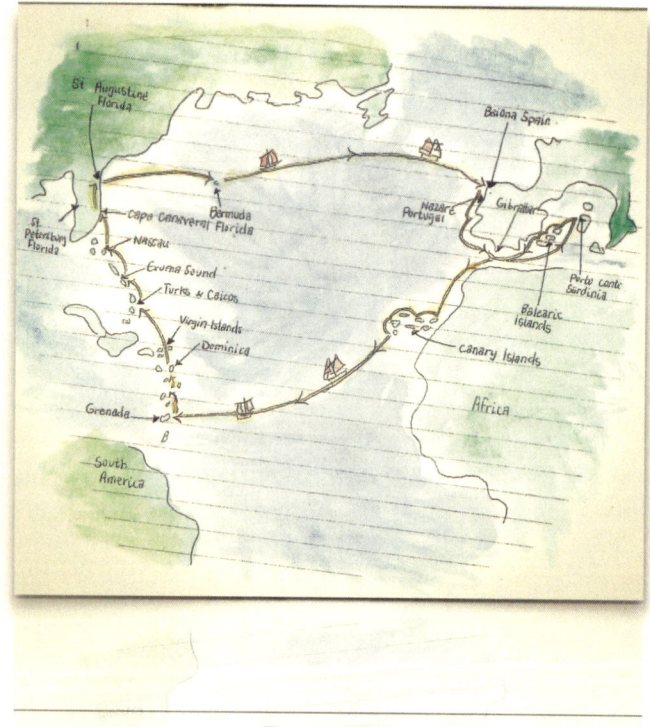

To view more pictures of Norna and

Kourtney's adventure, or to just write her a
message visit www.papersailor.com

Kourtney also has a Youtube video, please

subscribe to her channel and share!
www.youtube.com/user/accidentalsailorgirl

Thank you for reading.

165 & 166 ***

62, 68, 73